# Cognitive Virtual Assistants Using Google Dialogflow

Develop Complex Cognitive Bots Using the Google Dialogflow Platform

Navin Sabharwal
Amit Agrawal

Apress®

*Cognitive Virtual Assistants Using Google Dialogflow*

Navin Sabharwal
New Delhi, Delhi, India

Amit Agrawal
Mathura, India

ISBN-13 (pbk): 978-1-4842-5740-1
https://doi.org/10.1007/978-1-4842-5741-8

ISBN-13 (electronic): 978-1-4842-5741-8

Managing Director, Apress Media LLC: Welmoed Spahr
Acquisitions Editor: Celestin Suresh John
Development Editor: Matthew Moodie
Coordinating Editor: Aditee Mirashi

Cover designed by eStudioCalamar

Cover image designed by Freepik (www.freepik.com)

Distributed to the book trade worldwide by Springer Science+Business Media New York, 233 Spring Street, 6th Floor, New York, NY 10013. Phone 1-800-SPRINGER, fax (201) 348-4505, email orders-ny@springer-sbm.com, or visit www.springeronline.com. Apress Media, LLC is a California LLC and the sole member (owner) is Springer Science + Business Media Finance Inc (SSBM Finance Inc). SSBM Finance Inc is a **Delaware** corporation.

For information on translations, please e-mail rights@apress.com, or visit http://www.apress.com/rights-permissions.

Apress titles may be purchased in bulk for academic, corporate, or promotional use. eBook versions and licenses are also available for most titles. For more information, reference our Print and eBook Bulk Sales web page at http://www.apress.com/bulk-sales.

Any source code or other supplementary material referenced by the author in this book is available to readers on GitHub via the book's product page, located at www.apress.com/978-1-4842-5740-1. For more detailed information, please visit http://www.apress.com/source-code.

Printed on acid-free paper

*Dedicated to the people I love and the God I trust.*
*—Navin Sabharwal*

*Dedicated to my family and friends.*
*—Amit Agrawal*

# Table of Contents

# About the Authors

**Navin Sabharwal** has 20+ years of industry experience and is an innovator, thought leader, patent holder, and author in the areas of cloud computing, artificial intelligence and machine learning, public clouds, DevOps, AIOPS, DevOps, infrastructure services, monitoring and management platforms, big data analytics, and software product development. Navin is responsible for DevOps, artificial intelligence, cloud lifecycle management, service management, monitoring and management, IT ops analytics, AIOPs and machine learning, automation, and operational efficiency of scaled delivery through lean ops, strategy, and delivery. He is reachable at navinsabharwal@gmail.com and https://www.linkedin.com/in/navinsabharwal.

**Amit Agrawal** is a principal data scientist and researcher delivering solutions in the field of AI and machine learning. He is responsible for designing end-to-end solutions and architecture for enterprise products. He is reachable at agrawal.amit24@gmail.com and https://www.linkedin.com/in/amit-agrawal-30383425.

# About the Technical Reviewer

 **Neha Anand** is a cognitive solution architect. She is experienced in managing the delivery lifecycle of enterprise cloud and cognitive solutions. She has implemented and worked on chatbots using various cognitive engines such as Watson, LUIS, LEX, Dialogflow, etc. She has done conversational modeling using natural language processing as well as machine learning building on bots and worked in development and integration environments. Neha develops avenues to drive end-to-end solutions and leverage cognitive, artificial intelligence, and machine learning solutions. She is reachable at NehaAnand0511@gmail.com and https://www.linkedin.com/in/neha-anand-05.

# Acknowledgments

To my family, Shweta and Soumil, for being always there by my side, for letting me sacrifice your time for my intellectual and spiritual pursuits, and for taking care of everything while I was immersed in authoring this book. This and other accomplishments of my life wouldn't have been possible without your love and support. To my mom and my sister for the love and support as always; without your blessings, nothing is possible.

To my coauthor, Amit, thank you for the hard work and quick turnarounds to deliver this book. It was an enriching experience, and I look forward to work with you again soon.

To all my team members who have been a source of inspiration with their hard work, their ever-engaging technical conversations, and their technical depth. Your always-flowing ideas are a source of happiness and excitement every single day. Piyush Pandey, Sarvesh Pandey, Amit Agrawal, Vasand Kumar, Punith Krishnamurthy, Sandeep Sharma, Amit Dwivedi, Gauarv Bhardwaj, Nitin Narotra, Divjot, and Vivek: thank you for being there and making technology fun.

To Celestine and Aditee and the entire team at Apress for turning our ideas into reality. It has been an amazing experience authoring with you, and over the years, the speed of decision-making and the editorial support have been excellent.

To all my other coauthors, colleagues, managers, mentors, and guides, in this world of 7 billion, it was coincidence that brought us together, but it has been an enriching experience to be associated with you and learn from you. All ideas and paths are an assimilation of conversations that I have had and experiences I have shared. Thank you.

## ACKNOWLEDGMENTS

Thank you goddess Saraswati, for guiding me to the path of knowledge and spirituality:

असतो मा साद गमय, तमसो मा ज्योतिर् गमय, मृत्योर मा अमृतम् गमय

*Asato Ma Sad Gamaya, Tamaso Ma Jyotir Gamaya,*
*Mrityor Ma Amritam Gamaya*

*Lead us from ignorance to truth, lead us from*
*darkness to light, lead us from Illusion to Reality*

# Introduction

This book provides clear guidance on how to use Google Dialogflow to develop a cognitive chatbot that simulates a conversation between the bot and the user. You will start by understanding the technology landscape and various use cases where Google Dialogflow can be used. Specifically, the first two chapters will take you through the basics of Google Dialogflow, use cases of Google Dialogflow, and various cognitive platforms/frameworks, before moving onto advanced concepts and hands-on examples of using Google Dialogflow. The next chapters provide integrations that enrich Google Dialogflow using sentiment analysis, a spellchecker, the Google knowledge base, weather APIs, etc. We conclude the book by providing you with a glimpse of what to expect in the future for Google Dialogflow.

and integrate with other services such as sentiment analysis, weather forecasting, and personality analysis. In this chapter specifically, you'll get an introduction to chatbots.

# Cognitive Virtual Assistants

Let's deep dive into the main topic of this book, cognitive virtual assistants. The term *assistant* can be defined as someone or something that can assist in performing a task or activity. *Virtual* means something that exists in the virtual world such as software. The term *cognitive* relates to human cognition: "the mental action or process of acquiring knowledge and understanding through thought, experience, and the senses." It covers aspects of intellectual functions and processes such as attention, generation of knowledge, evaluation, reasoning, problem-solving, decision-making, comprehension, and formation of language.

In other words, cognition is a human ability that helps us to acquire knowledge, perform all our mental functions, gain knowledge from an environment, and create new knowledge from that.

Some cognitive virtual assistants have some of these capabilities, but they may not be as accurate as a human being today. However, there are certain areas in which they are better than humans as they don't have the limitation of processing power. In addition, they have an ability to scale and communicate with millions of users simultaneously, which is not possible for a human being.

Let's now define what a cognitive virtual assistant (CVA) is. A CVA is a software agent that performs tasks either for humans or for machines based on text, voice, and visual input. It has an ability to understand the input provided, interpret it, perform step-by-step operations, and probe a user for missing information. As a result, it can either provide some information or execute an intended task. CVAs have the capability to understand conversation in a natural language and maintain the context of conversation to achieve the end objective.

Some CVAs can be configured to process or interpret voice commands, images, and videos, and then perform an action accordingly. CVAs can respond in various formats depending on a mode of communication, i.e., text when the mode of communication is a messaging system, or voice to respond over voice channels. CVAs can also be embedded in devices such as speakers, navigation systems, and so on.

Nowadays, CVAs are available on multiple devices and interfaces and can be accessed via mobile handheld devices, laptops, and PCs. CVAs can also be integrated with various messaging platforms such as Facebook Messenger, Skype, Telegram, etc.

Virtual assistants can be leveraged to provide a variety of services. Here are a few examples:

- Virtual assistants can search various sources and retrieve information such as weather, stock updates, market information, prices, catalog information, interest rates, etc.

- Virtual assistants can act as a search engine to find relevant documents from document repositories.

- Virtual assistants can play videos or music from catalogs and subscription services such as Spotify, Netflix, Amazon Prime, etc.

- Virtual assistants can act as IT service desk agents to resolve problems and issues with IT equipment.

- Virtual assistants can conduct specialized services such as healthcare, legal, administrative, and finance functions.

- Virtual assistants can act as embedded agents in devices such as speakers, televisions, and other equipment.

- Virtual assistants can act as agents in vehicles to aid in navigation and operate entertainment devices like music players, etc.

# Use Cases for Cognitive Virtual Assistants

The following are use cases for cognitive virtual assistants.

## Self-Service/Help Desk for IT Services

Help desks for IT services that use cognitive virtual assistants are a way to reduce the effort of IT help-desk teams. In today's highly competitive environment, it is important to reduce the cost of delivering IT services while managing the efficiency of delivery.

Due to the 24/7 availability of CVAs and the ability to communicate with multiple users simultaneously, it is possible to respond to users whose requests have been waiting to be fulfilled. Users can also solve most of their issues or problems on their own through laptops, desktops, e-mails, and other enterprise applications via the self-service capabilities of CVAs.

Some mundane tasks such as resetting passwords and creating users can be easily achieved by CVAs, thus freeing up IT resources to work on more complex problems.

Some bots even come as ready-to-use IT use cases for faster adoption. One such bot framework is DRYiCE Lucy, which provides hundreds of out-of-the-box use cases for IT; see `https://www.dryice.ai/`.

# Triage

There are lot of use cases that fall in the triage category. CVAs in this category can ask users about issues and then route them to the right information or to the right agent for a resolution to the problem.

Interactive voice response (IVR) systems are an example of triage CVAs where they can ask the user to select an option over a telephony network and either provide information based on the option selected or route the user to a human agent. The IVR system of a telecom company, a broadband company, or a bank is a good example of how triaging works.

Organizations can use CVA capabilities to enable IVR to perform more intelligent communication and thus elevate the user experience. In fact, intelligent CVAs can understand a user's requirements and provide relevant information faster than IVR systems. Tasks such as retrieving account balances and security balances can be easily implemented by integrating CVAs with enterprise applications.

# Lead Generation

Lead generation CVAs are generally embedded within web sites. When a user visits any page of the organization's web site, a pop-up window for a CVA opens and starts a conversation with the user. These days you will find that most web sites have started using CVAs in a lead generation function to enhance the user experience.

With the help of CVAs, a user can get to know the information quickly and doesn't have to go through the entire web site navigating from page to page to find it.

In this use case, since a user is communicating with the CVA, they are an active user providing meaningful information through chat conversations that later can be used as a lead, for feedback, etc.

# E-commerce

E-commerce virtual assistants are most common types of CVA, helping millions of consumers to browse and select relevant products or services according to their preferences, within an intuitive interface.

It is difficult for users to search for products and services out of the millions of products that are currently available. However, with the use of advanced machine learning capabilities, CVAs not only converse with a user but can search relevant information to make buying and selling online easier.

E-commerce CVAs can have capabilities such as search and ranking algorithms to promote some products over others per a customer's requirements.

CVAs can be also be used to provide product offers to consumers, thus meeting a consumer's expectations and leading them to buy a product. This isn't the case if there is a static web site where the price of a product remains constant.

# Google Ecosystem

Google provides a set of enterprise-ready artificial intelligence (AI) services, applications, and tooling. It is a collection of cloud services running on the Google Cloud Platform. For example, Google uses the Natural Language API to identify insights from a large amount of unstructured text data. Google AutoML leverages the latest AI technologies to find an optimal model architecture for specific datasets to perform specific tasks. This section provides details of these AI services, which can be used for the development of various AI-based use cases.

# Google AI Platform

The Google AI Platform provides various cognitive services to make the usage of AI platforms easy for application developers. Specifically, it provides various cloud-based services, many pretrained models, support for new model training, and enterprise support. Google's AI Platform helps developers and data scientists to build machine learning products and move them from the proof of concept (PoC) stage to production. It mostly covers domains related to preprocessing, natural language, machine learning, and deep learning. These services are quite efficient and easy to implement in any environment.

# Products and Services

The following are some of the products offered as part of the Google AI Platform.

## Google Dialogflow

Google Dialogflow is one of the services from the Google Compute Platform that makes it easy for developers to develop and integrate cognitive virtual agents with their applications. It uses natural language understanding and natural language processing capabilities to build complex use cases. Because of the rising demand of chatbots to improve customer support and experience, Google Dialogflow offers technologies to develop robust and intuitive bots that can be launched across multiple chat channels, for example, Google Assistant, Line, Hike, etc.

## Google Natural Language API

The Google Natural Language API provides many pretrained models to be used for variety of natural language tasks such as sentiment analysis, entity recognition, etc. The huge corpuses over which the models are trained provide high efficiency and ease of direct predictions without the need to train the model. If the domain knowledge exploited in the dataset is peculiar or rather idiosyncratic, one can train their own model, though. The Natural Language API comprises five services, described next.

## Syntax Analysis

This service helps in the linguistic analysis of any text by generating part of speech tags, dependency trees, etc.

## Sentiment Analysis

This service helps in generating the sentiment score of a text. The service returns two main things.

- **Score**: The score is on a scale of -1 to +1 where the negative scale shows negative emotion, the positive scale shows positive emotion, and 0 is neutral.

- **Magnitude**: This is a value measuring the impact or strength of an emotion. If text is reinforcing an emotion, the score for magnitude will be high as compared to text with a plain visible sentiment and no reinforced emotion, although both might be equal scored.

## Entity Analysis

This service helps identify important entities such as places, locations, etc., with a confidence score that tells you how relevant an entity is to the identified phrases from given text. A higher score speaks of a higher importance of an entity with respect to the text.

### Entity Sentiment Analysis

This service helps identify the emotions that might be associated with each identified entity to give a better picture and analysis of text.

### Text Classification

This service helps classify the text into predefined categories and subcategories.

## Cloud AutoML

Cloud AutoML provides an end-to-end solution for applying machine learning to real-world problems. It allows developers to focus on tuning parameters specific to their dataset instead of developing workflows; hence, it is mostly concerned with data acquisition and prediction.

## Google Cloud ML Engine

The Google Cloud ML Engine enables developers and data scientists to build, deploy, and run their own machine learning applications in a serverless environment. It supports popular machine learning/deep learning frameworks such as Tensorflow to train your own model. It also has built-in tools support for better visualization and understanding of models.

## Google Tensorflow

Google Tensorflow is the enterprise version of Tensorflow for developing large-scale machine learning or deep learning applications with long-term support. It helps data scientists to design their own machine learning pipeline for any custom requirement and deploy it using the Google Cloud ML Engine.

# Data Labeling

A labeled dataset is required to solve most real-world problems, but labeling datasets correctly can be tedious. Data Labeling is Google's solution that helps you label a dataset with human labelers when you provide an annotation specification set and instructions. It uses state-of-art technologies such as proactive learning to capture label information from users and apply it to labeling an unlabeled dataset. The dataset you receive is labeled and can be easily used with the machine learning models it is required to train.

# AI Platform

The AI Platform basically is the solution to ease the ML development. For machine learning development, a lot of steps are involved, from idea to deployment; the AI Platform has an integrated tool chain to help you with the steps. It helps you build portable ML pipelines to implement on any environment with minimal changes. It has incorporated technologies such as Tensorflow, and Kubeflow to develop and implement solutions on the Google Cloud Platform and deploy them across environments.

# Cloud Talent Solution

Have you ever been looking for a solution that can search for relevant candidate profiles for a particular job posting? Google's Cloud Talent Solution will do this for you. It performs job search and candidate profile matching using natural language understanding and machine learning to understand candidate profiles and job postings to find relevant jobs for job seekers and relevant profiles for employers. These features have been released as an API, which can be leveraged to build a job search interface.

## Cloud Translation

Google's Cloud Translation service translates text between two languages. It leverages Google's pretrained language translation model to provide results as per the best model. The Cloud Translation service is easy to integrate into applications, web sites, tools, etc. It is generally used to provide multilingual capabilities to any application where building the machine learning model from scratch is a time-consuming and resource-intensive activity.

## Cloud Vision

Google Cloud offers two vision products: the Vision API and AutoML Vision. The Vision API provides pretrained machine learning models that automatically classify images with predefined labels, and AutoML Vision helps you to build your model with your own training labels. The cloud vision services provide solutions to current problems of using a computer with impaired vision, i.e., searching for products on an e-commerce web site and identifying emotions on human faces for emotion analysis. They also provide pretrained models to identify the faces of most popular celebrities.

## Video Intelligence

The Google Cloud Platform offers two video AI products: the Video Intelligence API and the AutoML Intelligence API. The Video Intelligence API provides pretrained machine learning models that automatically derive insights from stored or streaming video and help you to build your own model to derive insights based on your labeled dataset. Google's Video Intelligence API has been gaining popularity because of its applicability in different use cases such as video search engines, identification of a particular scene from video, etc.

**CHAPTER 2**

# Introduction to Google Dialogflow

Dialogflow is a natural language understanding platform from Google that helps developers to design conversational interfaces and integrate them into their applications. Dialogflow can be integrated with other cognitive services such as sentiment analysis, knowledge base services, etc. Dialogflow can also leverage cognitive, AI, and other services available from other cloud providers through API-based integration.

Google Dialogflow has built-in integrations available for common messaging platforms such as Facebook Messenger, Slack, etc. This enables developers to rapidly create chatbots that are integrated with popular messaging platforms.

In this chapter, we will discuss the key aspects to consider while designing cognitive chatbots using Google Dialogflow such as intents, entities, responses, parameters, etc.

## Example: Human-to-Human Interactions

In a chatbot system, a *conversation* is defined as communication between parties in which news or information is exchanged, questions are asked or answered, etc. We will start with an example of a sample conversation between users and demonstrate how a chatbot system recognizes the intent of the user.

© Navin Sabharwal, Amit Agrawal 2020
N. Sabharwal and A. Agrawal, *Cognitive Virtual Assistants Using Google Dialogflow*,
https://doi.org/10.1007/978-1-4842-5741-8_2

The following example shows the communication between a user who wants to travel and a support person who is supporting the user in booking travel-related services:

> *User: Hi, I am looking for some travel options from Pittsburgh to Boston. Can you help?*
>
> *Support Person: Sure! I will help you. How do you want to travel?*
>
> *User: I want to travel via flight.*
>
> *Support Person: When do you want to travel?*
>
> *User: October 30, 2019*
>
> *Support Person: OK. Which airline do you prefer?*
>
> *User: I will go with American Airlines.*
>
> *Support Person: That's nice. Below is the most relevant option available for your request.*
>
>> *Source City: Pittsburgh*
>>
>> *Destination City: Boston*
>>
>> *Date: October 30, 2019*
>>
>> *Departure Time: 10 a.m. EDT*
>>
>> *Arrival Time: 11:30 a.m. EDT*
>
> *User: Thanks! Please go ahead with the bookings.*
>
> *Support Person: Your flight ticket has been booked. Below are your itinerary details.*
>
>> *Source City: Pittsburgh*
>>
>> *Destination City: Boston*
>>
>> *Date: October 30, 2019*

*Departure Time: 10 a.m. EDT*

*Arrival Time: 11:30 a.m. EDT*

*PNR Number: 12345671*

This conversation between a user and a support person is quite common in travel-related conversations. Now, if we implement a chatbot to take the place of the support person, the chatbot will perform the following activities to have an interactive, human-like conversation with the user:

1. Identify the intention of user (i.e., look for travel-related information).

2. Extract location entities from the user's question (i.e., Pittsburgh and Boston). These are entities of type *location*.

3. Ask follow-up questions about the mode of travel.

4. Extract the entity for the type of travel mode (i.e., *flight* from user's response).

5. Ask a follow-up question about the day of travel.

6. Extract a date from the user's response.

7. Ask a follow-up question about the airline preference.

8. Extract the airline preference from the user's response.

9. Use the intent and entities to get flight information by calling the third-party API.

10. Respond to the user with flight information and ask for confirmation.

11. Process the confirmation message from the user and call the third-party API to book the tickets.

12. Respond to the user with the booking information.

Though these activities look complicated and beyond the capabilities of automated systems, with the advanced conversational capabilities being made available by machine learning technologies, it is possible to create such complex use cases. In subsequent sections, we will take a step-by-step approach to creating a conversation system using the Google Dialogflow engine.

# Building Your First Bot Using Google Dialogflow

Let's go through the steps for creating a conversation interface using Google Dialogflow. Let's start by creating a Google Dialogflow account. Please note that you should have a Google account before proceeding with the following steps. If you do not have a Google account already, you can sign up for one using the details at `https://accounts.google.com/SignUp`. Once you have a Google account, you can proceed to the next steps.

## Creating a Google Dialogflow Account

Follow these steps to create a Google Dialogflow account:

1. Go to `https://dialogflow.com/` and click the "sign for free" button.

2. The site will ask you to log in with a Google account.

3.  Select a Google account for setting up a Dialogflow
    account. After selecting an account, the site will ask
    you for the password for the selected account.

4.  After entering the password, you will be redirected
    to the confirmation screen where you need to accept
    the terms of service, as shown in Figure 2-1.

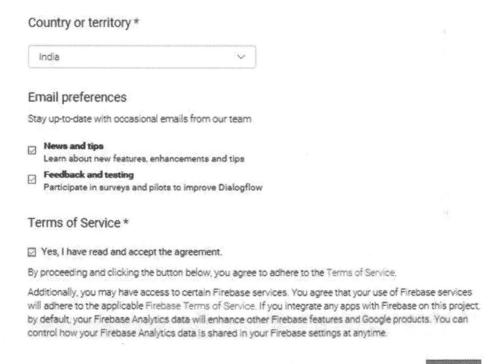

# Please review your account settings

Country or territory *

India

Email preferences

Stay up-to-date with occasional emails from our team

☑ **News and tips**
Learn about new features, enhancements and tips

☑ **Feedback and testing**
Participate in surveys and pilots to improve Dialogflow

Terms of Service *

☑ Yes, I have read and accept the agreement.

By proceeding and clicking the button below, you agree to adhere to the Terms of Service.

Additionally, you may have access to certain Firebase services. You agree that your use of Firebase services
will adhere to the applicable Firebase Terms of Service. If you integrate any apps with Firebase on this project,
by default, your Firebase Analytics data will enhance other Firebase features and Google products. You can
control how your Firebase Analytics data is shared in your Firebase settings at anytime.

ACCEPT

***Figure 2-1.*** *Agreement confirmation*

After reviewing and accepting the terms of service, you will be
redirected to the welcome page of Google Dialogflow, as shown in
Figure 2-2.

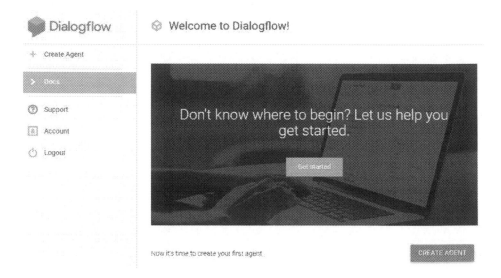

**Figure 2-2.** *Google Dialogflow welcome page*

# Using the Dialogflow Agent

The Dialogflow agent is a virtual agent that controls the end-user conversation. It implements natural language understanding technology to deduce the meaning of a human query. It converts natural language text or voice into a structured format that is used as input to an application, service, or third-party API.

An agent can also be defined as a collection or repository of use cases for a particular domain. Ideally, only one agent should be configured for use cases related to one domain. We need to create separate agents for use cases related to other domains. A domain in this context is an industry or vertical domain such as IT, healthcare, banking/financial services, etc.

An agent can also use the Google knowledge base if Dialogflow is not able to answer the user's query. The knowledge base acts as a searchable document store that can search documents by automatically extracting the intent from a user conversation and matching it to a document in the knowledge base. This feature is in beta at the time of writing of this book. Google Dialogflow can be enriched by enabling other features such as sentiment analysis, spellcheckers, and knowledge bases using agent configurations.

An agent can also use either a rule-based system or an ML+rule-based system for intent recognition. For example, we can use a rule-based system if fewer variations are available and can use an ML system otherwise. A rule-based system does not need a large amount of data to train a machine learning model; it simply uses rules that we configure to find the intent from the conversation.

Now, we will proceed to create an agent and configure it for the travel domain.

Click the Create Agent option in the top-left menu to add an agent, as shown in Figure 2-2. Provide the agent name, agent language, project description, and default time zone. Then click the Create button next to the agent name, as shown in Figure 2-3. We will simply name our agent **Travel** as we are going to create a use case for the travel industry.

*Figure 2-3.* *Creating an agent*

We will be redirected to the screen shown in Figure 2-4.

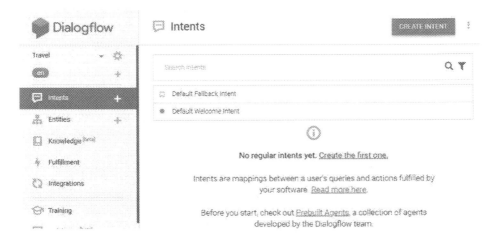

***Figure 2-4.*** *Use case design*

# Defining the Intents and Entities

Before creating the intents, let's first discuss some of basic concepts related to Google Dialogflow.

## Use Case

A *use case* is a complete end-to-end conversation flow for a scenario. It includes all the possible paths that the system can take to provide a relevant response to the query asked by a user. A simple example is something like *Tell me about travel options from Pittsburgh to Boston.* The conversation system will recognize the intent, entities, and actions, and it may also trigger your webhook APIs to provide responses to your queries by integrating with third-party systems that may have this data. In Google Dialogflow, a single intent or collection of intents can be referred to as the *use case*.

# Intent

An *intent* is the verb or action that is part of the conversation with the user. Dialogflow categorizes end-user inputs into the relevant intent. In each agent, a user can define multiple intents, with the combined intents controlling the flow of a conversation. For each intent, we can specify how to respond to the user based on the use case. As an example, an intent for a query from a user saying *Tell me about travel options from Pittsburgh to Boston* would be Travel since the user is looking for some information related to travel.

For example, in Figure 2-5, one of scenarios shows that if the user says *Tell me about travel options from Pittsburgh to Boston*, Dialogflow triggers the Travel intent. Also, it extracts the useful parameters from the user input. Thus, the first step in a conversation workflow is the ability of the system to extract the intent. The intent is the most important element in the conversation flow; if the system is unable to extract the intent and match it, the workflow wouldn't meet its end objective of solving the question or query of the user. As we proceed through the chapters in this book, we will learn how to fine-tune the system to extract the intents clearly, handle scenarios where there may be ambiguity in intent, and use the best practices for configuring our system so that the accuracy of our agent in handling users' intents is satisfactory.

*Figure 2-5.* *Use case design flow*

Intents contain the information covered next.

## Training Phrases

For each intent, the *training phrases* are the set of sample utterances from the end users of our use case. Google Dialogflow uses these phrases to train built-in machine learning algorithms for intent classification. These examples should be captured from end users who are using the system or will use the system. The data from previous chats and paths that user queries took will come in handy to train Google Dialogflow. Chat logs, manual standard operating procedures, call logs, web logs, web form requests, e-mails, etc., will contain information on how the user conversation flow happens and what queries customers are asking related to this use case and domain. The training phrases are also called *utterances*. This is the end-user data that is used to train the machine learning models so that the model can then accurately determine the intent when a new question is asked by a user by matching it to the already configured training phrases. Readers should note that the training phrases or utterances are not matched one to one with the query that the user is asking, but these are used to train a model, and thus the agent will be able to correctly figure out the intent even if a user's query is different than any of the training phrases configured in the system. Google Dialogflow uses machine learning and natural language understanding and processing models to figure out the intent. Thus, it is important for a cognitive virtual assistant developer to understand use cases, intents, training phrases, and entities in depth to be able to configure the use case correctly and provide the correct response to new queries.

## Action Field and Parameters

When an intent is matched, the Action field value is defined by us, and this value is passed on to the fulfilment webhook requests or APIs. In other words, the action is used to trigger the logic in the workflow.

Parameters, entities, values, and responses are defined under an action, and they are used to extract the required information from the user to complete the workflow, as shown in Figure 2-6.

We can define various parameters as required, which will ensure that the agent will ask the user for this information in a step-by-step fashion as explained in our use case example and will proceed to fulfilment only once all the required information has been extracted in the conversation. After getting all the required data, the agent can then query an external system through a webhook API to provide information or lodge a fulfilment request in the external system. In the case of our travel example, the required information about the source destination, location destination, date and time of travel, and mode of travel are important elements that are needed for the agent to complete the use case.

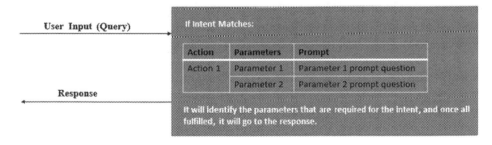

***Figure 2-6.***  *Action and parameter*

As an example, the parameter values from a user query *Tell me about travel options from Pittsburgh to Boston* are Pittsburgh and Boston. We can add parameters to the intent by clicking the New Parameter link. You need to provide the following details for each parameter, as shown here:

- **Required**: Select this only if it is a mandatory parameter for an intent.

- **Parameter Name**: Set the name of the parameter. Example: source-city and destination-city.

- **Entity**: Define the system or developer entity for this parameter. Example: @sys.geo-city.

- **Value**: Define a variable where the parameter value will be stored. Example: $source-city and $destination-city.

- **Is List**: Specify whether this parameter should contain multiple values or not.

- **Prompts**: Regularly ask questions if relevant or required input was not provided. This field is used only if the Required field is selected. Example: Please Enter Source City.

The following example is configured with two parameters (i.e., source-city and destination-city) to extract the source and destination city from the sample query, as shown in Figure 2-7. Each of the parameter has been defined with the system entity @sys.geo-country. So, whenever there is an occurrence of the source and destination city in a query, these parameter values (i.e., Pittsburgh and Boston) will be extracted and stored in the variables $source-city and $destination-city, respectively. If the required parameters are missing, the chatbot will ask for more information with *Please enter source city and please enter destination city*. Once this information is entered, these variables can be used to generate dynamic responses in order to have an interactive conversation with the user. Here, the entity type defines how these parameter values will be extracted from end-user inputs. We will discuss entities in the subsequent section in detail; for the moment, just think of entities as object types and entity values as objects.

| REQUIRED ❷ | PARAMETER NAME ❷ | ENTITY ❷ | VALUE | IS LIST ❷ | PROMPTS ❷ |
|---|---|---|---|---|---|
| ☑ | source-cit | @sys.geo-city | $source-ci ty | ☐ | Please Ent er So... |
| ☑ | destinatio | @sys.geo-city | $destinati on-city | ☐ | Please Ent er De... |
| ☐ | Enter nam | Enter entit | Enter value | ☐ | ... |

+ New parameter

***Figure 2-7.*** *Parameters*

## Responses

Google Dialogflow supports built-in response handlers where we can configure a response for an intent. So, whenever the end-user expression matches the relevant intent and entities, the corresponding response will be displayed to the user. We can define different types of responses other than just text formats such as image, audio, speech, etc. The user can use parameter reference variables in the response field to generate a dynamic response. We can even define multiple responses for an intent to make our agent more human-like, where the agent will choose one of the responses at random.

In regard to the previous example, based on the earlier user query (i.e., *Tell me about travel options from Pittsburgh to Boston*), we captured two parameters: $source-city and $destination-city. We will configure these parameters in the following response text in the "Responses" section, as shown in Figure 2-8:

*It's nice you want to travel from $source-city to $destination-city.*

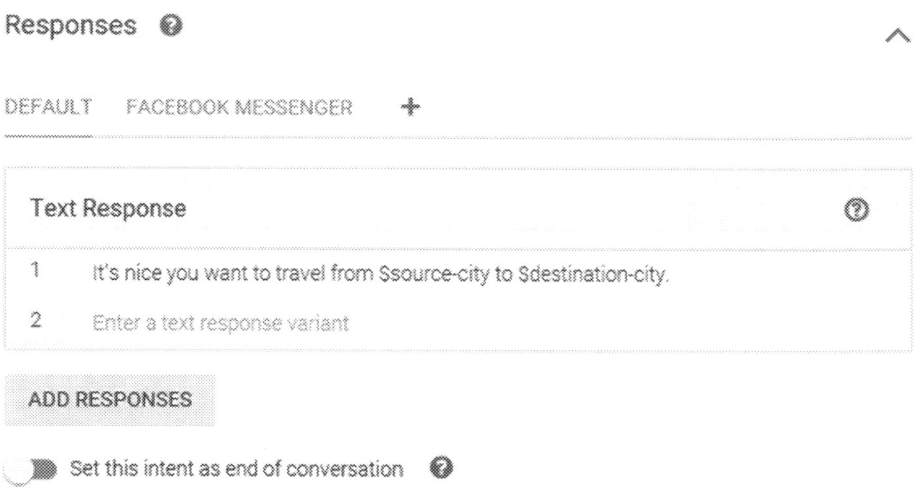

Responses ❓                                                                    ⌃

DEFAULT    FACEBOOK MESSENGER    ✛

| Text Response | ❓ |
|---|---|
| 1    It's nice you want to travel from $source-city to $destination-city. | |
| 2    Enter a text response variant | |

ADD RESPONSES

⬤▶ Set this intent as end of conversation  ❓

***Figure 2-8.*** *Response*

Here, the captured value of $source-city and $destination-city will be
Pittsburgh and Boston, respectively, as per the user expression. Hence,
the user will see the response *It's nice you want to travel from Pittsburgh to
Boston.* We can also make our conversation more human-like by creating
multiple responses like this:

> *Have a safe trip, you want to travel from $source-city to
> $destination-city.*

Figure 2-9 shows the basic flow of intent matching.

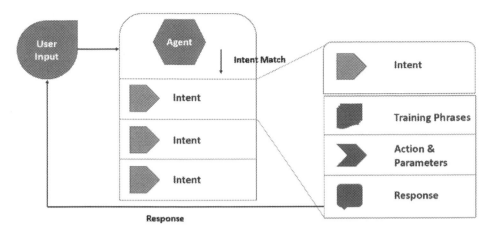

***Figure 2-9.*** *Intent matching flow*

# Entities

*Entities* are nouns that combine with the intent to identify a particular action. An entity also specifies how parameter values will be extracted from user expressions. In the previous example, the system entity (@sys. geo-city) is used to extract the parameter values (Pittsburgh and Boston). Each parameter has an entity type, which shows what type of data is to be extracted and stored in the parameter value.

## System Entities

Google Dialogflow provides a set of predefined *system entities* such as @sys.email, @sys.number, @sys.phone-number, etc. Dialogflow enables system entities automatically if a training phrase has one of these entities, as shown in Figure 2-10.

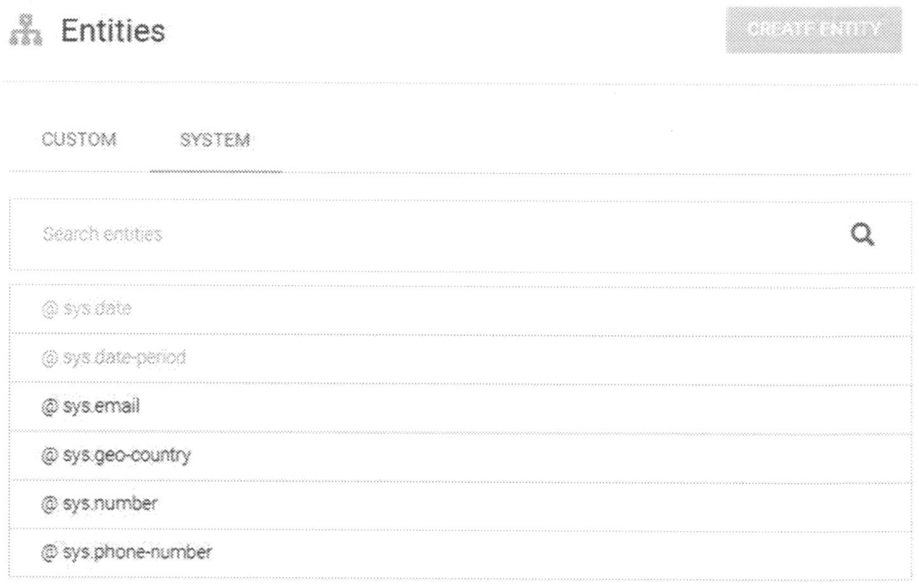

*Figure 2-10.* *System entities*

## System Entity Extension

Dialogflow provides a set of predefined entities to extract the information from end-user expressions. But for most use cases, it may require extra values that are not predefined by Dialogflow. We can extend system entities for this purpose. In the Training Phase section on the intent page, we can add values to a system entity by annotating a training phase.

## Regexp Entities

Dialogflow provides features for defining regular expressions as entity entries. This is useful if the user wants to extract or recognize entity entries from user expressions that follow certain patterns such as for a phone number, e-mail address, country, etc. For example, if we want to define a regular expression to extract an e-mail address, then we can define the regular expression **^[\w.]**+@[a-zA-Z_]+?\.[a-zA-Z]{2,3}$, as shown in Figure 2-11.

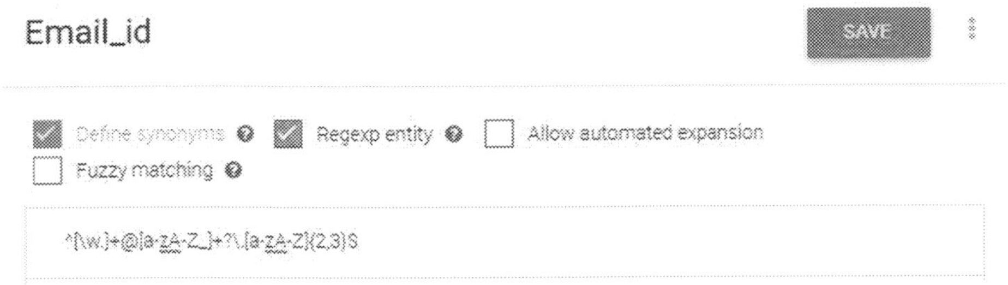

Email_id                                              SAVE         ⋮

☑ Define synonyms ❷   ☑ Regexp entity ❷   ☐ Allow automated expansion
☐ Fuzzy matching ❷

^[\w.]+@[a-zA-Z_]+?\.[a-zA-Z]{2,3}$

***Figure 2-11.*** *Regexp entities*

## Referencing Entity Values and Synonyms in the Training Phrases

Since we'll be defining the entities and values related to the variations, we can add entity values or synonyms in the variations to create a relation mapping between the intents and the entities. Returning to the previous example, say we want to add the variations related to travel options. We have an entity called *@sys-geo-country* with entries such as Pittsburgh and Boston, so we can add these values as part of the variations. Figure 2-12 shows some examples of such variations.

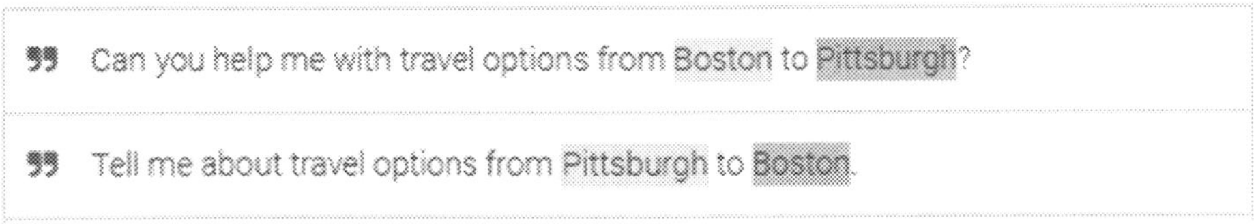

❯❯ Can you help me with travel options from Boston to Pittsburgh?

❯❯ Tell me about travel options from Pittsburgh to Boston.

***Figure 2-12.*** *Variations*

## Batch Operations

Dialogflow provides the ability to copy, move, and delete multiple entities using batch operations, as shown in Table 2-1 and Figure 2-13.

29

***Table 2-1.*** *Batch Operations*

| Operation | Description |
| --- | --- |
| Copy | This is used to transfer the selected entities into the destination agent without removing any in the current agent. |
| Move | This is used to transfer the selected entities into the destination agent and remove any from the current agent. |
| Delete | This is used to delete the selected entities permanently from the agent. |

CUSTOM     SYSTEM

☐                                           COPY        MOVE        DELETE        CANCEL

☑  Airlines

☐  Travel_option

***Figure 2-13.*** *Batch operations*

# Testing the Intents

After defining the intents and variations, we can test them in the Google Dialogflow "Try it now" panel available on the right side of the agent configuration page, as shown in Figure 2-14. And we can see, the intent is triggered based on the variations added, and the correct response has been populated.

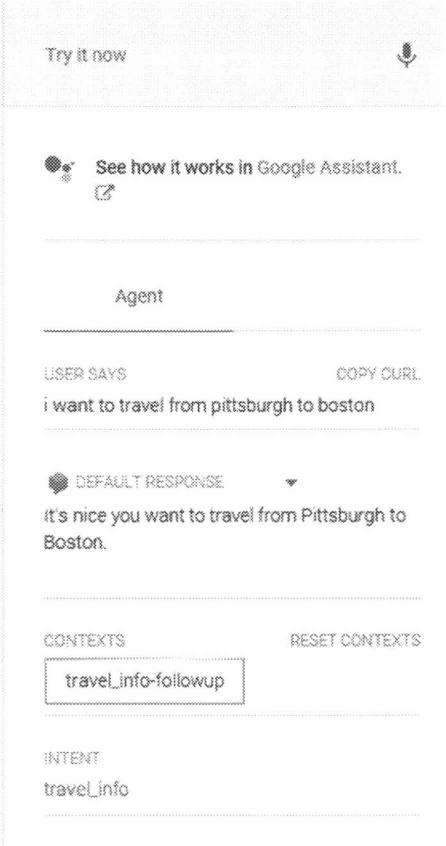

*Figure 2-14.*  *"Try it now" panel with correct response*

We have explained the basic concepts of Google Dialogflow that are necessary for training a conversation system. Let's now create a use case in a step-by-step manner.

We will start with the identification of a use case. For this example, we are continuing with the use case from the travel domain that we have used in the previous examples.

The chatbot system can be integrated with a travel web site where users can log in and start conversing with our chatbot system. As an example, the user wants to travel from one place to another. The user is looking for travel options such as train, flight, etc., and the cognitive bot will capture the intent of the user and decipher what it is.

You can download the agent zip file that has the use cases configured for the travel domain. Go to https://github.com/dialogflow34/Chat-Bot/tree/master/Chapter_2 to download the Create_First_Bot.zip file.

Once you have downloaded the agent, you can import it into Google Dialogflow.

Let's see how to import a precreated agent into Google Dialogflow.

1.  Go to the Settings page and then click Export and Import; Dialogflow will redirect you to the page shown in Figure 2-15.

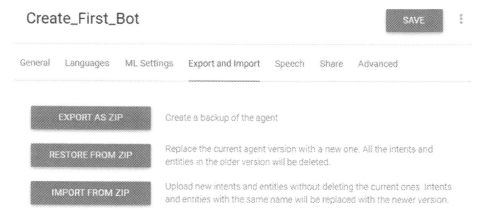

***Figure 2-15.*** *Exporting and importing a zip file*

2.  Click IMPORT FROM ZIP, upload the Create_First_Bot.zip file that you downloaded, and type IMPORT. Then click Import, as shown in Figure 2-16.

You can upload an agent as a zip archive consisting of the folders "intents" and "entities" and a file called "agent.json". The folders should contain JSON files of the intents and entities. In the agent.json file you can include agent settings such as language, enabled domains, default time zone, match mode, and ML classification threshold.

Important:
Intents and entities that you upload will replace existing intents and entities with the same name.

Drop files here to attach them
or
SELECT FILE

Create_First_Bot.zip

IMPORT

IMPORT    CANCEL

*Figure 2-16. Importing an intent*

3. Once you click Import, the agent will be imported to Google Dialogflow. Then go to the Intents page, where you can see the intent for the travel use case, as shown in Figure 2-17.

Intents                                      CREATE INTENT

Search intents                                    Q  Y

Default Fallback Intent

Default Welcome Intent

Travel_info

*Figure 2-17. Intents page*

Once we have identified a use case to work upon, we will move on to the intent, training phrases, entities, and response configuration.

# Working with Intents

The following sections explain how to work with intents.

## Default Intent

By default, Dialogflow has two intents, named Default Welcome Intent and Default Fallback Intent, as shown in Figure 2-18.

*Figure 2-18.*  *Default intents*

- **Default Welcome Intent**: This intent is triggered when the user starts a conversation with the bot. The intent gives a response to the user with the information about what your agent does. This is the first response from the bot to the user.

- **Default Fallback Intent***: This intent is triggered if no condition is matched in any of the intents in the hierarchy. If the workflow matches the condition of any other intent, this intent is not executed. Thus, if none of the intents is matched, the agent can respond by gracefully exiting the conversation, as shown in Figure 2-19.

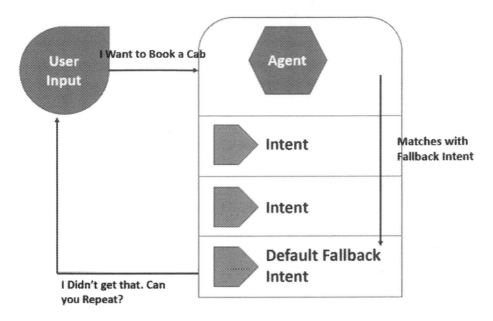

***Figure 2-19.*** *Fallback intent*

The user can add training phrases explicitly to the default fallback intent that will act as negative examples. In some situations, there may be similar sentences, but they may not match with the intent; these negative example variations will ensure that the intent is matched correctly and excludes the negative training variations.

## Create and Train a New Intent

Let's create and train a new intent named Travel_info. The entity parameters are as follows:

- **Entity type**: Travel_option
  - **Entity entries**: Train, Flight
- **Entity type**: Airlines
  - **Entity entries**: American Airlines, JetBlue

With the previous information, next we need to define utterances or training phrases that the user might ask when using the bot, as shown here:

> *I want to book a flight from Chicago to San Francisco*
>
> *I want to explore tourism options in Las Vegas*
>
> *Help me with travel options from Las Vegas to Brooklyn*
>
> *Travel options from Chicago to Boston*
>
> *I want to travel from Los Angeles to San Francisco*

Ideally, in a practical scenario, these phrases should be collected from end users to provide actual variations to the system for training.

Let's move on to creating an intent with training phrases, entities, and responses.

- Log in to the Google Dialogflow console.

- Select the agent named Travel that we created earlier.

- In the top-left menu, click the + sign next to Intents. Provide **Travel_info** as the intent name and click the Save button, as shown in Figure 2-20.

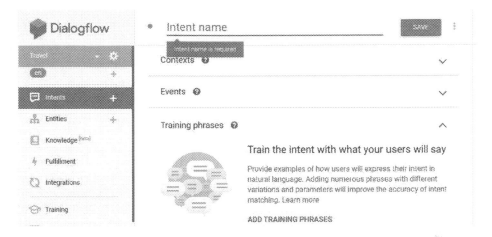

**Figure 2-20.**  *Creating an intent*

- Click the drop-down menu next to "Training phrases"
  and then click the ADD TRAINING PHRASES link to
  add possible user utterances, as shown in Figure 2-21.

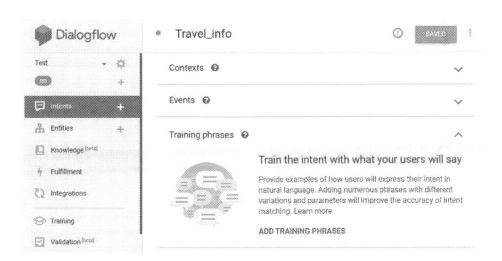

**Figure 2-21.**  *Going to the training phrases*

- Enter training phrases or user utterances one by one
  and press Enter. These are the sample variations that
  we will feed into the Google Dialogflow engine for
  training. Google Dialogflow will automatically annotate
  entities to relate variations with intents, as shown in
  Figure 2-22.

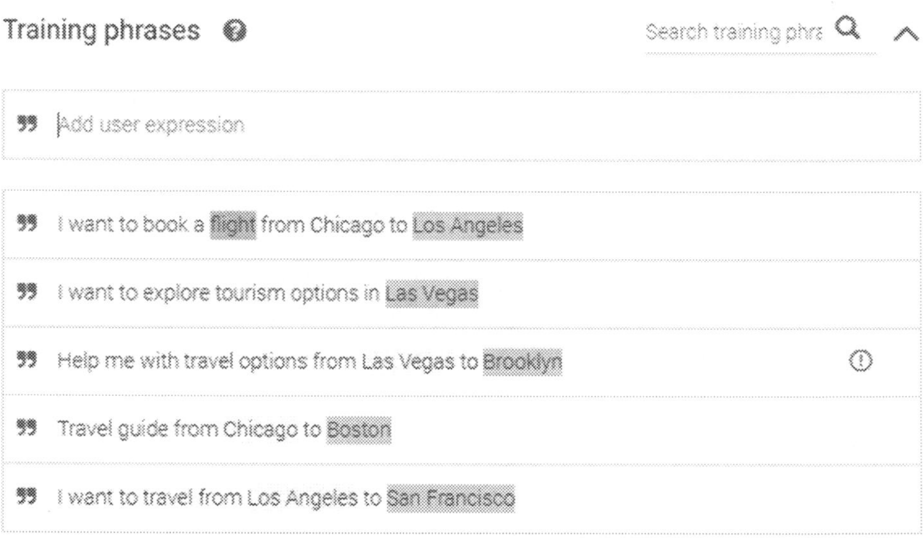

*Figure 2-22.*  *Adding training phrases*

As per best practices, please ensure the following criteria are met while configuring training phrases:

- Add at least ten examples/variations or more as
  training phrases for an intent. The more variations, the
  better the training, and that results in better responses
  from the bot.

- Two different intents shouldn't have similar types of
  training phrases. This is required to avoid any kind of
  overlap during intent recognition.

Dialogflow provides limited types of system entities. To match any custom data, the user can create a developer entity such as Travel_option. Follow these steps:

1. Go to the left menu of the agent and click the Entities tab. Then click CREATE ENTITY.

2. Fill in the entity name at the top of the page. This defines the type of information the user wants to extract from the query. Enter **Travel_Option** as the name here.

3. Click the first row and enter an entity value and synonym. Here, enter **Flight** with a synonym of **Flight**.

4. Like previously, fill in the next rows as per the requirements, as shown in Figure 2-23. Here, enter **Train** with a synonym of **Train**.

After entering these values, your screen will look like Figure 2-23.

The "Allow automated expansion" option is used to match the entity values that are explicitly defined in the developer entities. If the user mentions some value that is not included but similar to an entity, then this feature recognizes the value as a parameter in the entity.

The "Fuzzy matching" option is used if the user wants to enable the matching of incorrectly spelled entity entries from user expressions. Google Dialogflow uses built-in machine learning and natural language processing algorithms for fuzzy logic. You can select these options or leave them unchecked.

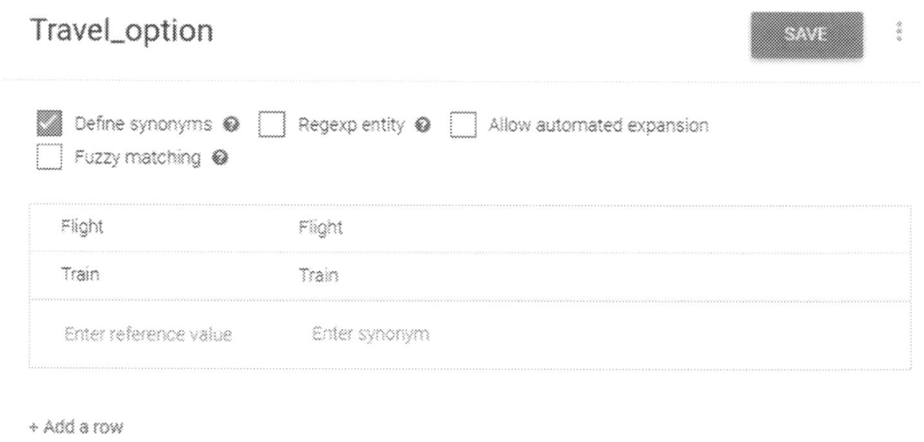

Travel_option                                                    SAVE    ⋮

☑ Define synonyms ❷    ☐ Regexp entity ❷    ☐ Allow automated expansion
☐ Fuzzy matching ❷

| Flight | Flight |
| Train | Train |
| Enter reference value | Enter synonym |

+ Add a row

***Figure 2-23.***  *Entity Creation*

# Defining an Action and Parameters

Now we will configure an action and parameters so that we can extract the relevant entities from the conversation and prompt the user appropriately.

Configure the parameters for our use case as per Table 2-2. Then we will discuss the configuration of these parameters.

*Table 2-2.* *Action and Parameters*

| S. No. | Required | Parameter Name | Entity | Value | Is List | Prompts Text |
|--------|----------|----------------|--------|-------|---------|--------------|
| 1 | Yes | source-city | @sys.geo-city | $source-city | No | *Please enter source city.* |
| 2 | Yes | destination-city | @sys.geo-city | $destination-city | No | *Please enter destination city.* |
| 3 | Yes | Travel_options | @Travel_option | $travel_option | No | *That's nice. Please tell me how you want to travel.* |
| 4 | Yes | airlines | @Airlines | $airlines | No | *Please mention airline.* |
| 5 | Yes | date | @sys.date | $date | No | *Please mention date.* |

For each parameter, configure the following properties:

- **Required**: Check this for all parameters. This restricts users to providing values for all the parameters.

- **Parameter Name**: Provide the name of all parameters as mentioned in Table 2-2 in the column "Parameter Name."

- **Entity**: This defines which entity entries will be stored in a particular parameter. For our use case, define the entity as per Table 2-2.

- **Value**: This is a variable that stores values of entities from a user's query. For our use case, define variables as per Table 2-2 in the "Value" column.

- **Is List**: Define whether a parameter can have multiple values. For our use case, each parameter will have only a single value. Hence, don't select this option for any parameter.

- **Prompts**: A text message will be prompted to the user if values of parameters are not provided by the user. Please note that this will be enabled if you select the Required option for a parameter.

Once configured, your system should look like Figure 2-24.

We can configure the prompts for each parameter by clicking the "Define prompts" link in the Prompts column for each of the required parameters, as shown in Figure 2-24.

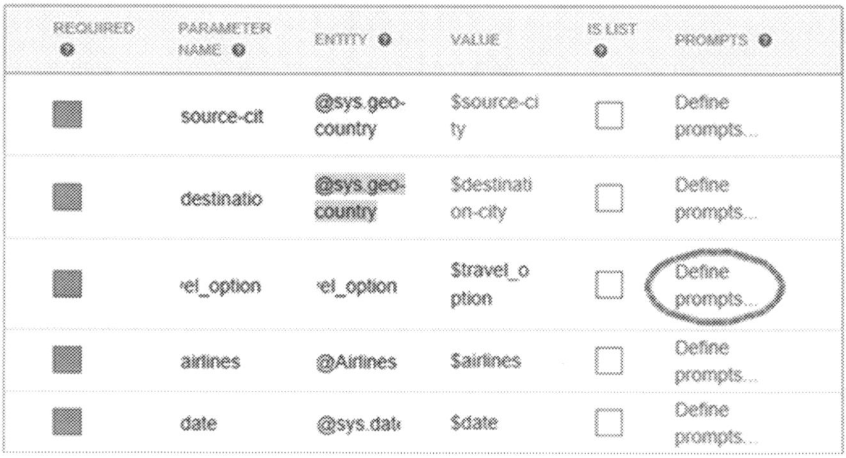

*Figure 2-24.*  *Defining a prompt message*

This opens a new window to define your own prompt text for the parameter **Travel_**option, as shown in Figure 2-25. Define a prompt for the parameter Travel_option as **That's nice. Please mention how you want to travel.** and click the Close button.

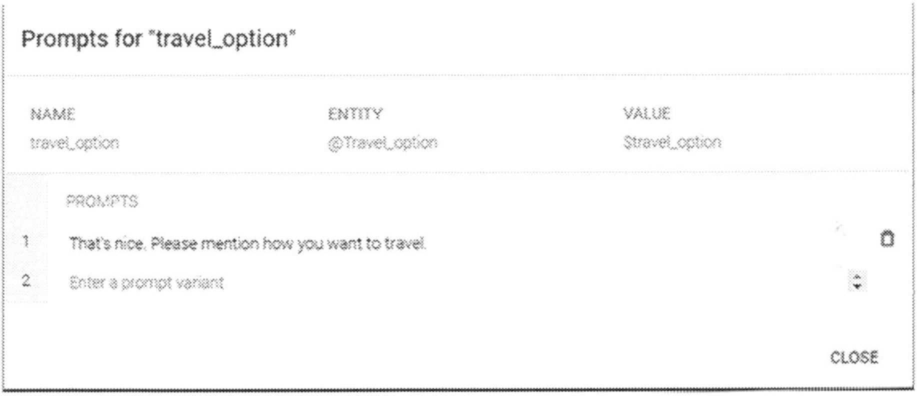

*Figure 2-25.* *Prompt configuration*

For this use case, configure the prompt text for all the parameters as per the details shown in Table 2-2. The "Action and parameters" fields will look like Figure 2-26. After defining all the parameter prompts, click the Save button next to the intent name to save the changes to the "Action and parameters" configuration.

The required parameters ensure that the agent will ask the queries to probe the users for additional information until all the required information is captured.

Once all the required parameters are filled in, then the parameter values can be used to either provide the final response to the user as configured in the system or use webhooks to query external APIs to provide the response; if the agent fails to match the intent and entities, then the fallback response is provided to the user.

Action and parameters                                                  ∧

| REQUIRED ● | PARAMETER NAME ● | ENTITY ● | VALUE | IS LIST ● | PROMPTS ● |
|---|---|---|---|---|---|
| ☑ | source-cit | @sys.geo-city | $source-ci ty | ☐ | Please Ent er So... |
| ☑ | destinatio: | @sys.geo-city | $destinati on-city | ☐ | Please Ent er De... |
| ☑ | travel_opti | @Travel_o ption | $travel_op tion | ☐ | That's Nic e. Pl... |
| ☑ | airlines | @Airlines | $airlines | ☐ | Please me ntion ... |
| ☑ | date | @sys.date | $date | ☐ | Please me ntion ... |
| ☐ | Enter nam | Enter entit | Enter value | ☐ | ... |

***Figure 2-26.*** *"Action and parameters" fields*

# Defining the Responses

Now, we can configure the response by clicking the drop-down button next to the Response section for the intent Travel_info. Define the response message as follows:

*Your $airlines flight ticket has been booked. Below is your itinerary details. Source City: $source-city Destination City: $destination-city Date: $date Departure Time: 10:00 AM EDT Arrival Time: 11:30 AM EDT PNR Number: 12345671*

In the response message, parameter values are used to generate dynamic responses (i.e., $airlines, $source-city, and $destination-city).

For this use case, we have hard-coded the values for the departure time, arrival time, and passenger name record (PNR) number to show how a response should be configured. Click the Save button to save the response message, as shown in Figure 2-27. Here, we can add any type of message such as images, speech, or messages from other third-party messaging platforms.

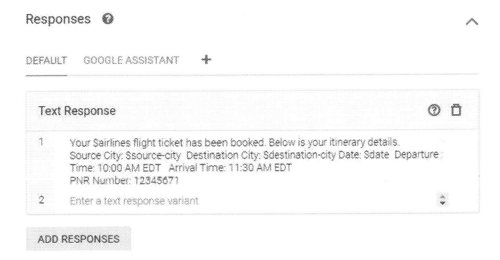

*Figure 2-27.  Configuring a response*

We have configured intents, entities, parameters, and responses for the Travel_info use case. Google Dialogflow automatically starts training the agent as soon as an intent and its complete details have been configured.

Next, we need to test whether our configured use case is working well. For that, go to the test console, and at the top-right corner of the Dialogflow console, enter the query **I want to travel from Log Angeles to San Francisco**. Then click the Enter key, as shown in Figure 2-28.

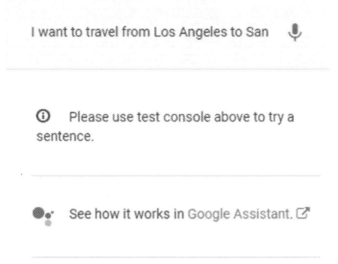

**Figure 2-28.**  *Testing in the "Try it now" panel*

Dialogflow will send the query to the agent, which in turn classifies the user expression to the relevant intent (i.e., the Travel_info intent) followed by identifying the entity entries of type @sys.geo-city (a system entity). Since the user hasn't specified the mode of travel and other parameters in the initial query, the Dialogflow agent will prompt the user with the defined prompt text for the other parameter values, as shown in Figure 2-29, Figure 2-30, Figure 2-31, and 2-32.

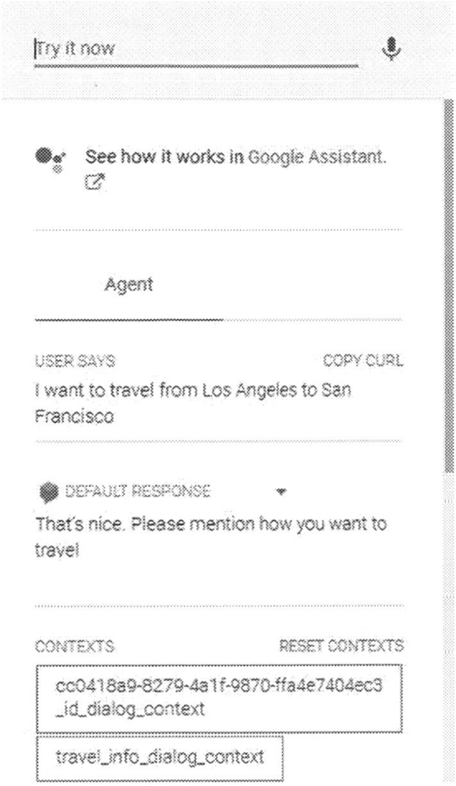


***Figure 2-29.*** *Test console*

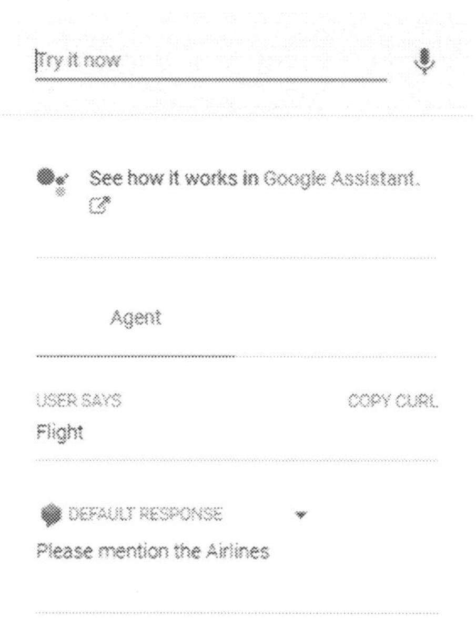

Try it now

See how it works in Google Assistant.

Agent

USER SAYS                                    COPY CURL
Flight

DEFAULT RESPONSE        ▾
Please mention the Airlines

*Figure 2-30.*  *User Prompt - Airline*

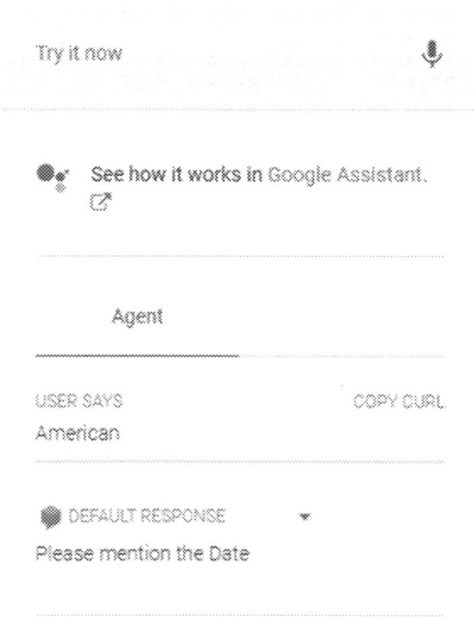

Try it now

See how it works in Google Assistant.

Agent

USER SAYS                                    COPY CURL
American

DEFAULT RESPONSE        ▾
Please mention the Date

*Figure 2-31.*  *User Prompt - Date*

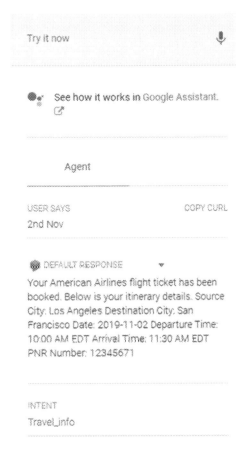

*Figure 2-32.*  *Flight Booking Confirmation*

# Integrating with the Built-in Bot Framework Web Demo

Google Dialogflow provides a built-in bot known as Web Demo to which we can link our agent. To enable this integration, go to the top-left menu and click Integrations; then enable the Web Demo connector by clicking the toggle button, as shown in Figure 2-33.

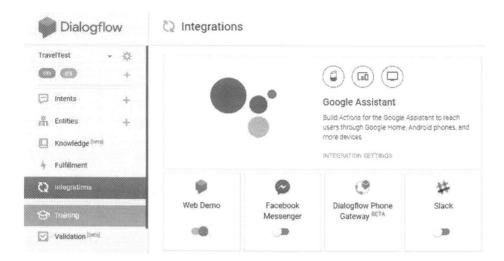

**Figure 2-33.**  *Integrating with Web Demo*

Once enabled, we can click the Web Demo icon. This takes us to the
Web Demo configuration screen. Now, we can see the Web Demo URL that
has been generated automatically for this agent, as shown in Figure 2-34.

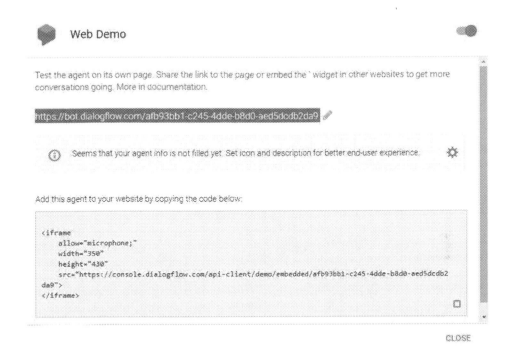

*Figure 2-34. Web Demo configuration*

# Trying Your First Bot

Copy the highlighted URL as shown in Figure 2-34 and open it in the browser of your choice; this will open the conversation window, as shown in Figure 2-35. Note that the URL for your system will be different than the URL shown here.

***Figure 2-35.***  *Web Demo conversation interface*

Now, we can try the use cases that we have configured in our Google
Dialogflow agent, as shown in Figure 2-36, Figure 2-37, and Figure 2-38.

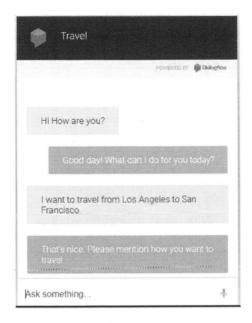

***Figure 2-36.*** *Web Demo - User's Query*

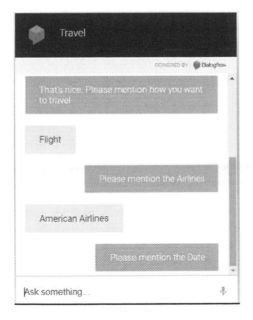

***Figure 2-37.*** *Web Demo - User Prompt*

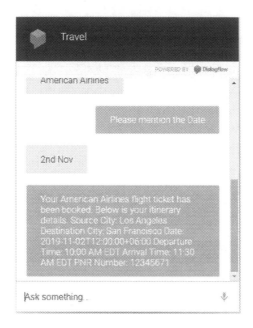

***Figure 2-38.*** *Web Demo - Flight Booking Confirmation*

# Conclusion

In this chapter, we designed our first cognitive chatbot using Google Dialogflow. We also discussed basic concepts such as intents, entities, parameters, etc., with an example to give you a glimpse at the building blocks that are essential to creating conversation use cases in Google Dialogflow.

# CHAPTER 3

# Advanced Concepts in Google Dialogflow

In previous chapter, we discussed how to create a simple chatbot. In this chapter, we will discuss advanced topics such as dialog context (input and output contexts), follow-up intents, multilingual bots, webhooks, and more. These advanced features will help us to configure complex use cases.

## Input and Output Contexts

In previous chapter, we configured a simple use case where we triggered a single intent (i.e., Travel_info) with actions and parameters defined as source-city, destination-city, Travel_options, airlines, and date with probing questions to extract the entity values from the conversation, as shown in Figure 3-1.

© Navin Sabharwal, Amit Agrawal 2020
N. Sabharwal and A. Agrawal, *Cognitive Virtual Assistants Using Google Dialogflow*,
https://doi.org/10.1007/978-1-4842-5741-8_3

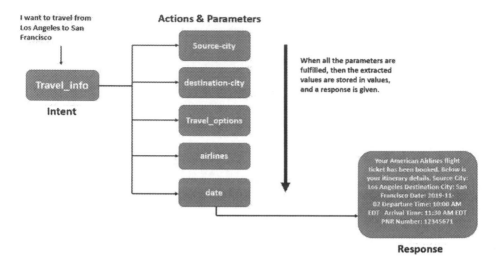

**Figure 3-1.** *Recap of action and parameters*

Now, let's take a step forward and imagine a scenario where a user might ask further questions based on the response of the previous intent. So, when the agent responds with *Are you looking for any other bookings?* the user might say *cab booking* or *accommodation* to continue a conversation flow. We'll create separate intents for these services, and the challenge is connecting these intents as part of the conversation flow with the first intent.

Dialogflow provides a feature called *input/output context* that controls the flow of conversation and branching. Contexts can be set for intents and can be reused further in other intents. Whenever an intent is created, we get two options: input and output contexts. For the first intent, we set the output context, and then every other intent that is to be linked to the first intent needs to have its input context defined to be the same as the output context of the first intent. This way, these two intents can be associated with each other. We can define multiple input and output contexts to configure more complex use cases.

We can use the context to keep track of the conversation state based on what intents match and to direct the conversation based on the user's previous response. Context also stores entity values and parameters for the already matched intent. Here are the two definitions:

- **Output context**: Dialogflow activates the output context after the intent is matched.

- **Input context**: The input context can be used to filter which intents are matched. An intent will be matched only if the specified input contexts are currently active. This means that the output context of the originating or previous intent is active.

To understand this, let's continue with the previous example wherein the agent gives the *Are you looking for any other bookings?* response. Here the output context of the intent Travel_info is set to Travel. So, every intent that has the context Travel that you set as its input is a potential intent that could be triggered. If the user gives the response *cab* or *hotel booking*, then to continue the flow of conversation, we need to set the input context in the cab and accommodation intents to be the same as the output context set in the Travel intent. This continues the conversation flow of the respective service, cab booking or hotel booking, as shown in Figure 3-2.

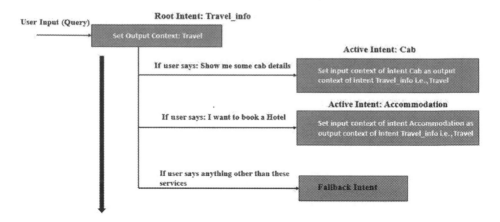

**Figure 3-2.** *Input and output contexts*

As shown in Figure 3-2, if the user asks a travel-related query, it will trigger the Travel_info intent, and then its output context will be set to Travel. Here, the Cab and Accommodation intents are going to activate as their input contexts are defined as the Travel context. Now, if the user asks cab- or accommodation-related questions, the respective intent will be triggered based on the user query matching with the training phrases defined in the intents. But if a user's query does not match any of the active intents, then it will go to the fallback intent.

You can download the agent that has the use case configured for the travel domain using the input and output contexts. Go to `https://github.com/dialogflow34/Chat-Bot/tree/master/Chapter_3` to download the `Travel_IO_context.zip` file.

Import the downloaded agent into Google Dialogflow, as explained in the Chapter 2.

Let's configure the use case where we will be showcasing how to link the cab intent with the Travel_info intent using the input and output contexts. As a first step, we'll define the output context as **Travel** for the first intent, Travel_info, that we created in the previous chapter, as shown in the Figure 3-3.

***Figure 3-3.*** *Output context, Travel_info*

Configure the cab intent with the following information, as shown in Figure 3-4 and Figure 3-5:

- **Intent**: Travel_Cab

- **Entity type**: Cab_Vendor

- **Entity entries**: Uber

- **Training phrases**:

  - *I want to book a cab from San Francisco airport to Parker guest house at 5pm*

  - *I want to travel to airport using Lyft*

  - *Show me some cab details*

  - *Cab services*

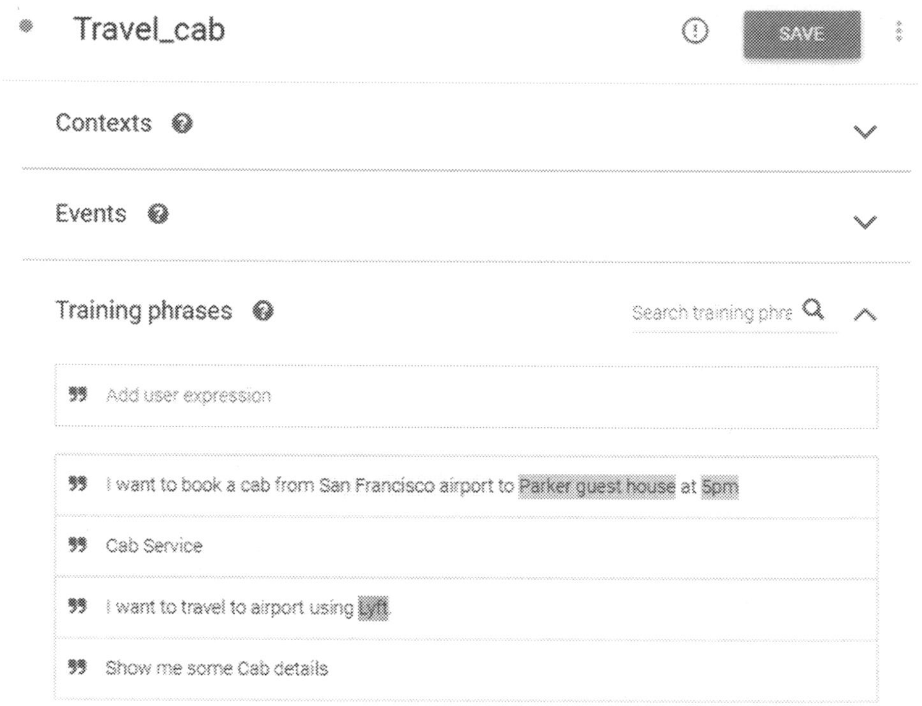

**Figure 3-4.** *Intent configuration, Travel_Cab*

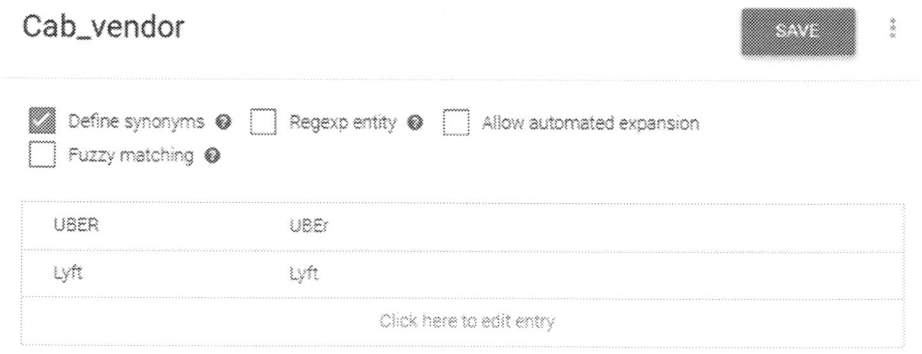

**Figure 3-5.** *Defining an entity, Travel_Cab*

Now, define the input and output contexts for the Travel_Cab intent. Click the drop-down menu next to the Contexts label. Then, enter the input context as **Travel**, which is the same output context of the Travel_ info intent, and enter the output context as **Cab**. Here, defining the output context for the intent Travel_Cab is optional, as shown in Figure 3-6. It is defined to include subsequent cases in upcoming sections.

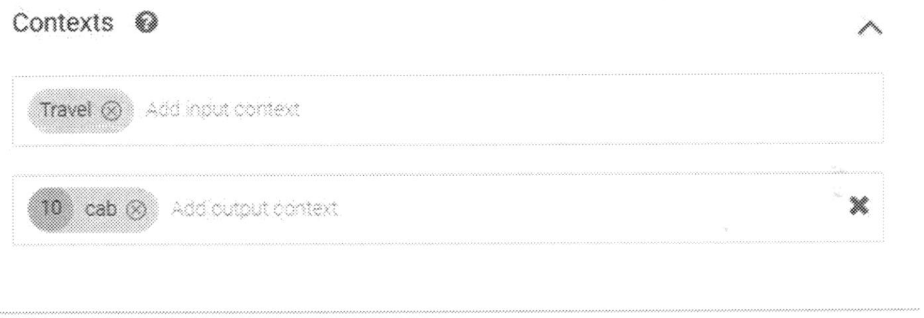

*Figure 3-6.* *Input and output contexts*

To book a cab, the agent will need some mandatory information from the user such as the source, destination, day and time of travel, and preferred cab vendor. This information can be asked of the user as per the configuration in the "Action and parameters" section of the intent Travel_ Cab, which is shown in Figure 3-7.

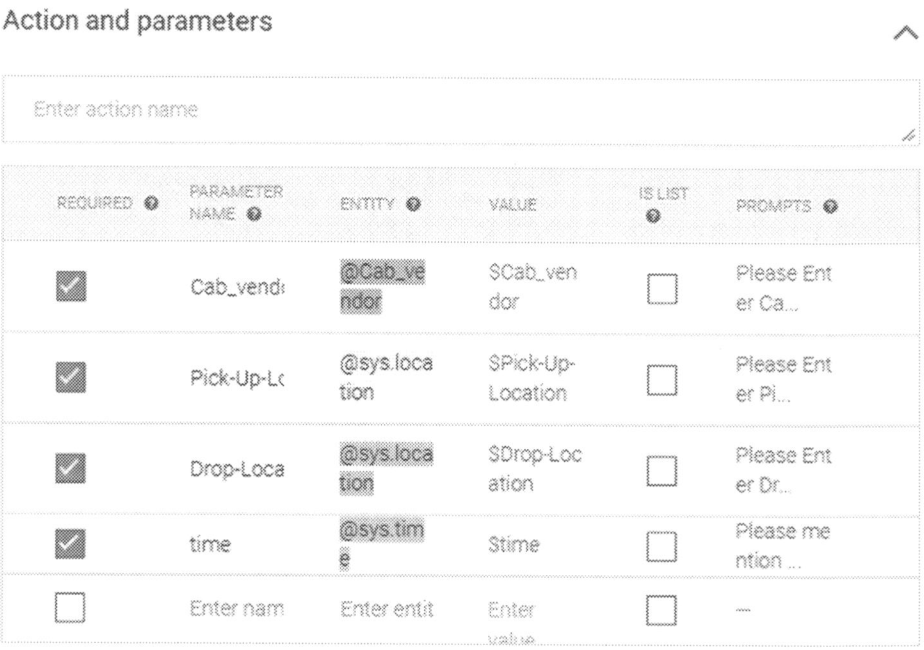

## Action and parameters    ⌃

Enter action name

| REQUIRED ❷ | PARAMETER NAME ❷ | ENTITY ❷ | VALUE | IS LIST ❷ | PROMPTS ❷ |
|---|---|---|---|---|---|
| ☑ | Cab_vendi | @Cab_ve ndor | $Cab_ven dor | ☐ | Please Ent er Ca... |
| ☑ | Pick-Up-Lc | @sys.loca tion | $Pick-Up- Location | ☐ | Please Ent er Pi... |
| ☑ | Drop-Loca | @sys.loca tion | $Drop-Loc ation | ☐ | Please Ent er Dr... |
| ☑ | time | @sys.tim e | $time | ☐ | Please me ntion ... |
| ☐ | Enter nam | Enter entit | Enter value | ☐ | --- |

***Figure 3-7.*** *"Action and parameters" page for Travel_Cab*

The values for the parameters Cab_vendor, Pick-Up-Location, etc.,
are being stored in variables that can be used in the Responses section
to make the bot more interactive. For example, the Text Response entry
in Figure 3-8 will generate custom messages based on the values of
parameters.

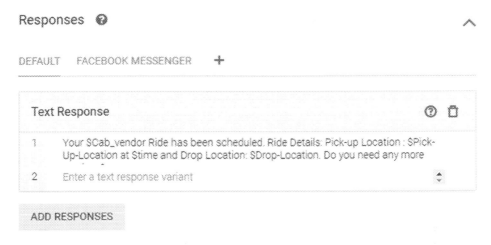

Responses ❓                                                                                    ⌃

DEFAULT    FACEBOOK MESSENGER    ✛

Text Response                                                                          ❓  🗑

1    Your $Cab_vendor Ride has been scheduled. Ride Details: Pick-up Location : $Pick-
     Up-Location at $time and Drop Location: $Drop-Location. Do you need any more

2    Enter a text response variant                                                         ⬍

ADD RESPONSES

***Figure 3-8.*** *Defining a response, Travel_Cab*

Click the Save button next to the intent name to save the changes. Now, you can try your chatbot configuration in the "Try it now" panel, as shown in Figure 3-9, Figure 3-10, and Figure 3-11.

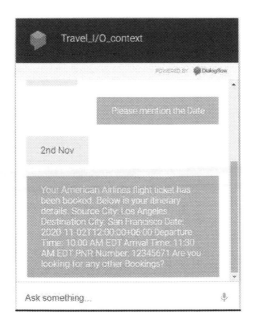

Travel_I/O_context

POWERED BY 🔷 Dialogflow

Please mention the Date

2nd Nov

Your American Airlines flight ticket has been booked. Below is your itinerary details. Source City: Los Angeles. Destination City: San Francisco Date: 2020-11-02T12:00:00+06:00 Departure Time: 10:00 AM EDT Arrival Time: 11:30 AM EDT PNR Number: 12345671 Are you looking for any other Bookings?

Ask something...                                                          🎤

***Figure 3-9.*** *I/O context use cases*

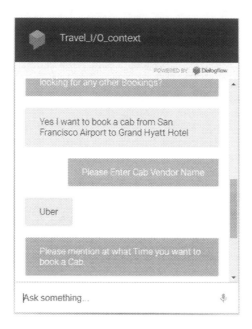

**Figure 3-10.** *I/O context use cases, continued*

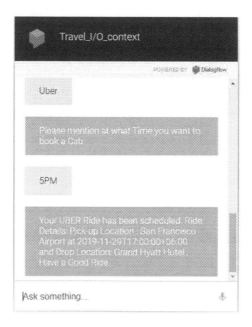

**Figure 3-11.** *I/O context use cases, continued*

# Follow-Up Intents

In "Input and Output Contexts" section, we discussed how multiple intents can be combined to form a conversation flow using contexts. However, Dialogflow provides a feature known as *follow-up intents*. A follow-up intent is like a child intent of the associated parent intent. Since it will be follow-up intent, all input and output contexts will be set automatically. The follow-up intent will be triggered only after the conversation has already matched with the parent intent in a previous conversation.

Now, what's the difference between the two if both of them are doing same thing?

If we use the follow-up intents feature, then the child intent would be triggered only after triggering the root intent. Please note that the child intent can't be triggered from any other intent available in the agent even if its input context has been set by that intent. However, if we use the input and output contexts, then follow-up intents can be triggered from any other intent available in the agent if the input context to the follow-up intent has been set by that intent, as shown in Figure 3-12.

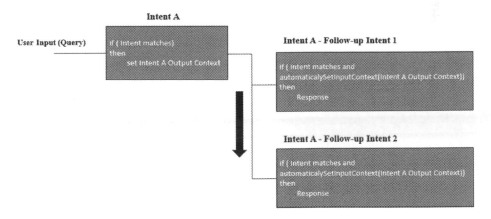

***Figure 3-12.*** *Follow-up intent*

As shown in the figure, if the user expression matches the training phrases of Intent A, then only their follow-up intents will be matched further, either Follow-up Intent 1 or Follow-up Intent 2. And their input contexts will be automatically set as the output context of the parent intent. Once the follow-up intent is matched, it will give a response.

You can download the agent that has the use case configured for travel using follow-up intents.

Go to `https://github.com/dialogflow34/Chat-Bot/tree/master/Chapter_3` to download the `Travel_Follow_up.zip` file.

Import the downloaded agent into Google Dialogflow, as explained in Chapter 2.

Next, we will configure same intents as defined in earlier sections (i.e., Travel_info and Travel_Cab) and connect them using the follow-up intents feature of Dialogflow. Configure the intent Travel_info in the same manner as defined in Chapter 2.

Now, right-click the intent Travel_info and select the "custom" option from the drop-down menu, as shown in Figure 3-13.

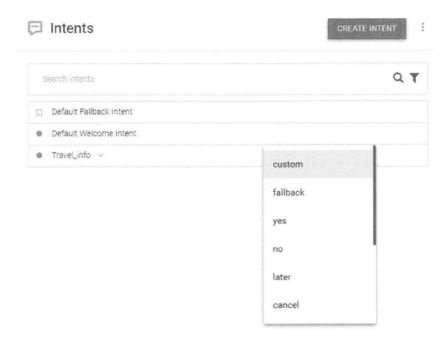

***Figure 3-13.*** *Custom follow-up intents*

This will create a custom intent with the name Travel_info-custom, as shown in Figure 3-14. Rename this custom intent to **Travel-cab**.

***Figure 3-14.*** *Custom follow-up intent named Travel-cab*

The output context (Travel-followup) of the Travel_info intent and the input context (Travel-followup) of the Travel-cab intent will be set automatically, as shown in Figure 3-15 and Figure 3-16.

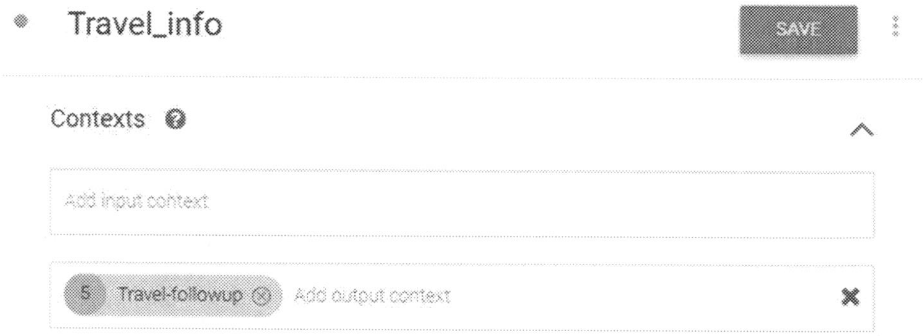

*Figure 3-15.* Follow-up intents, Travel_info

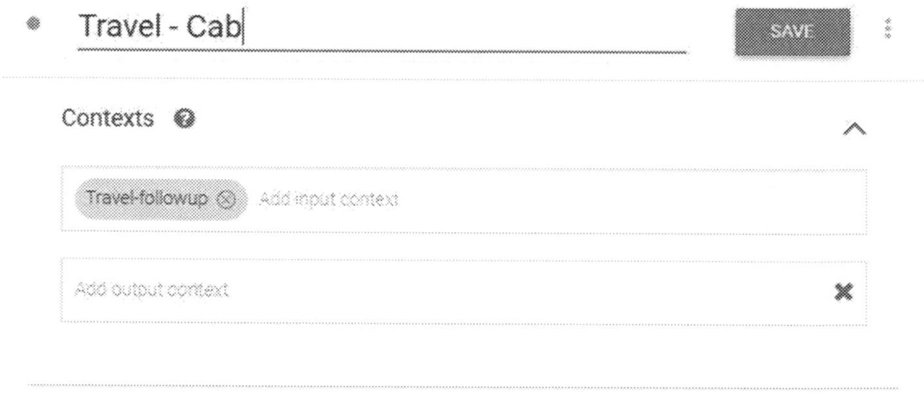

*Figure 3-16.* Follow-up intents, Travel-cab

Now, consider the scenario where the user is looking for either cab bookings or accommodations just after confirming the travel. In other words, either the cab booking intent or the accommodation intent should be triggered after the Travel_info intent.

The follow-up intents feature of Dialogflow can be used here to create a child intent (i.e., Travel_accommodation, with Travel_info being the parent intent). Follow the same method as defined earlier in this section to create the follow-up intent. Right-click the Travel_info intent and select "custom" in the drop-down menu; a new follow-up intent with the name Travel_info-custom will be created. Rename it to **Travel-accommodation** and click the Save button next to it, as shown in Figure 3-17.

*Figure 3-17.* *Custom intent, Travel-accommodation*

Next, you can see that the input context of the intent Travel-accommodation has automatically been set to Travel-followup, which is the output context of the parent intent Travel_info, as shown in Figure 3-18.

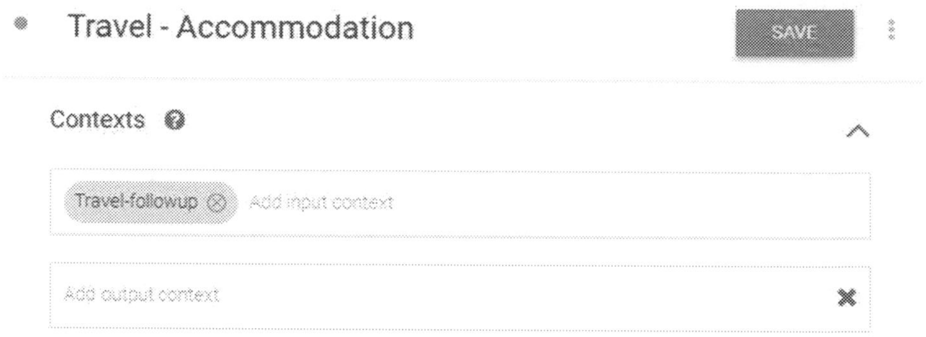

*Figure 3-18.*  *Follow-up intent, Travel-followup*

Now, configure other details of the Travel-accommodation intent as shown here:

- **Entity type**: Room_Type (Define Synonyms)

    - **Entity entries**: Single, Double

- **Entity type**: Duration (Regexp entity)

    - **Entity entries**: [1-9]+\s*nights\s*[1-9]+\s*days

- **Entity type**: Hotel_name

    - **Entity entries**: Hilton, Hyatt, Embassy Suites, Sheratons

- **Training phrases**:

    - *I need an accommodation.*

    - *I want to book a hotel.*

    - *What are the different hotels available?*

    - *I want to book single room in Hyatt hotel for 3 nights and 2 days.*

As we can see, the new entity type (i.e., the regexp entity) has been defined in this intent. It will be used to extract the duration of stay at a hotel from the user's query. It will identify patterns such as three nights, two days, etc., as shown in Figure 3-19.

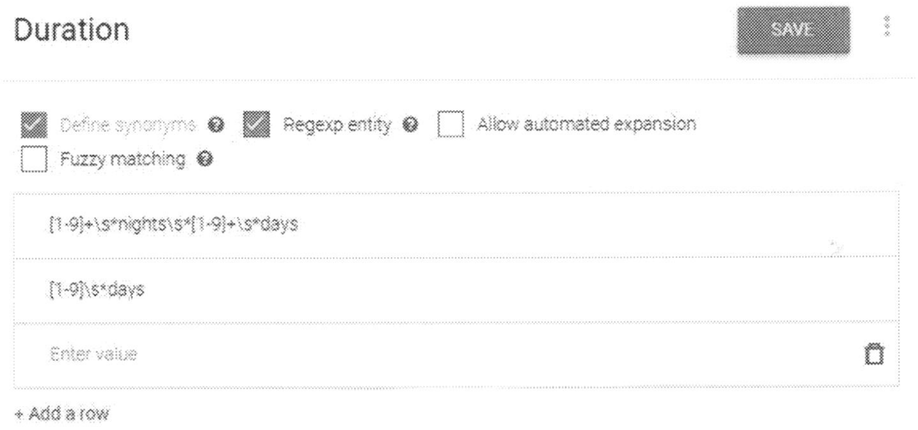

*Figure 3-19.* *Entity configuration, duration*

Next, configure the mandatory parameters such as Room_Type, Duration, Hotel_name, from-date, and to-date in the section "Action and parameters" of the intent Travel-accommodation. The trickiest part here is how to showcase values that have been captured in the root intent as part of the Responses section of the current intent. We can refer those values with a combination of the output context of that intent and the variable name where the information has been stored.

In the following example, destination-city has been captured from the root intent. For this, a combination of the input context (i.e., Travel-followup) and variable name destination-city is used as #Travel-followup. destination-city, as shown in Figure 3-20.

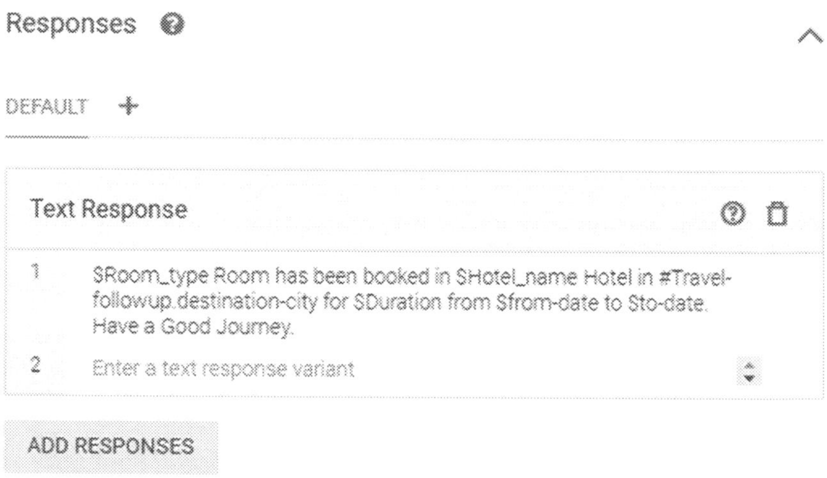

Responses
DEFAULT
Text Response
1 $Room_type Room has been booked in $Hotel_name Hotel in #Travel-followup.destination-city for $Duration from $from-date to $to-date. Have a Good Journey.
2 Enter a text response variant
ADD RESPONSES

***Figure 3-20.*** *Response*

Now, go to the top-left menu and click Integrations. Enable Web Demo, and it will show up as a link to your chatbot agent. Open it in a browser, and you can start conversation, as shown in Figure 3-21.

Travel
Please mention the Date
2nd Nov
Ask something...

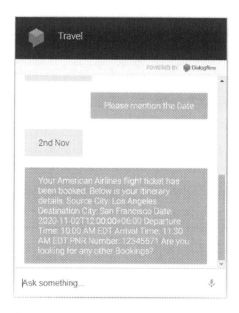

***Figure 3-21.*** *Travel use case*

In Figure 3-22, the user mentioned that he is looking for cab services, and accordingly the chatbot responded to the user's query.

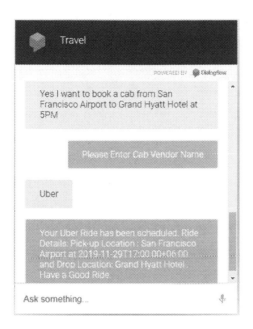

*Figure 3-22.* *Cab Booking Confirmation*

But this time, the user has also asked for accommodation services, and the chatbot responds accordingly, as shown in Figure 3-23 and Figure 3-24.

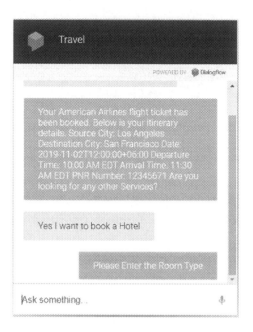

***Figure 3-23.***  *User Prompt - Room Type*

Once all the mandatory parameters are captured, the chatbot responds. Here, the destination-city San Francisco has been captured, as explained earlier using a combination of the context and variable name.

***Figure 3-24.*** *Hotel Booking Confirmation*

# Handling Multiple Intents (Intent Priority)

Dialogflow comes with a unique implementation to handle multiple intents, called *intent priority*. By default, all intents have a normal priority. If multiple intents have been recognized from a query, then we can set the priority, and the highest priority intent will be triggered.

For example, in the query I am traveling from the United States to the United Kingdom and I want to book a cab from the airport to the hotel. So, two intents (i.e., Travel_info and Travel_Cab) should be recognized, but the order of their execution matters. As per the defined use case, the Travel_info intent should be triggered first, and then Travel_Cab intent should be triggered. In this case, during configuration, the priority of the Travel_info intent should be set to higher than the Travel_Cab intent.

Consider a case where we have only two intents, Travel_Cab and Travel_info, as shown in Figure 3-25. For these intents, configure the options in "Action and parameters," the entities, and the responses, as mentioned in the previous sections.

*Figure 3-25.*  *Intent list*

Now, we will use the "Try it now" panel to see how our conversation system is responding with the default configuration (i.e., all intents at normal priority).

The user has entered the query *I want to travel from US to UK and I also want to book cab*. The chatbot has recognized both intents simultaneously, but because of a high confidence score of the Travel_Cab intent, it has triggered this intent before the Travel_info intent, as shown in Figure 3-26, where it is asking questions from the Travel_Cab intent instead of the Travel_info intent. Ideally, the Travel_info intent should be triggered first, before the Travel_Cab intent.

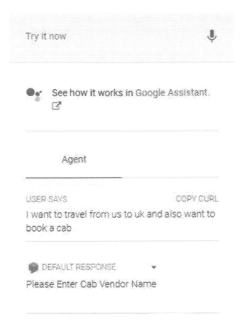

***Figure 3-26.*** *Handling multiple intents*

We can solve this problem by increasing the priority of the intent Travel_info from Normal to Highest. So, whenever two intents are being recognized from a single user's query and Travel_info is one of them, then it will always be triggered first.

To increase the priority of the intent Travel_info, click the circle icon (in red) just before the name of intent, as shown in Figure 3-27. Change the priority of the Travel_info intent to Highest.

**Figure 3-27.**  *Priority configuration, Travel_info*

Now, open the "Try it now" panel and enter the same query (i.e., *I want to travel from US to UK and I also want to book cab*). This time you can see the Travel_info intent has been triggered first, as shown in Figure 3-28. Please note that the Travel_info intent will always be triggered even if the user enters the query *I want to book cab and I also want to travel from US and UK*.

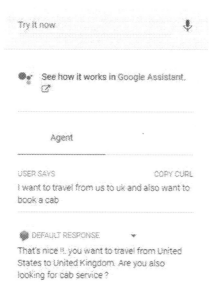

**Figure 3-28.**  *Handling multiple intents, Travel_info*

# Intent Training

Dialogflow's natural language processing is based on machine learning. To improve the performance of the agent, the user can add explicit training data. It provides an interface for incorporating both external and internal customer interaction logs into an agent's training phrases. You can use this feature to build a new Dialogflow agent using the logs of existing customer interactions and to improve the performance of a live Dialogflow agent using its own logs.

# Conversation List

Click the Training tab in the left sidebar menu. You will be redirected to the page that shows the list of conversations. The agent conversation log will automatically appear in the conversation list. You can also upload log data from other sources by uploading the text data, as shown in Figure 3-29.

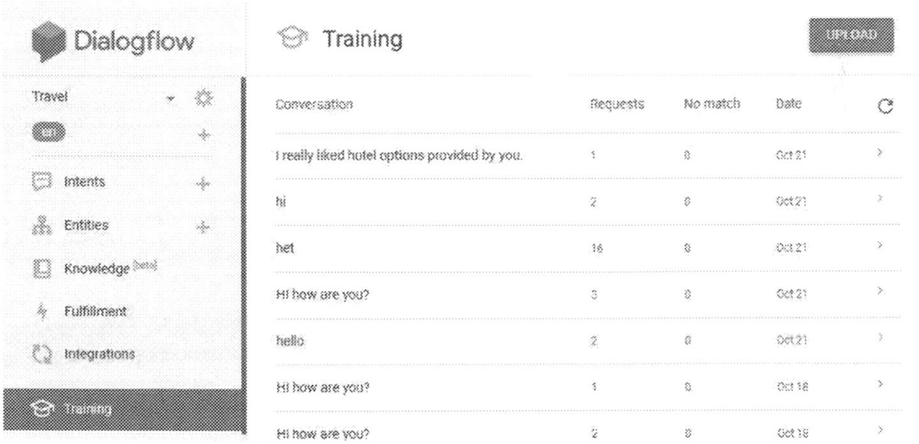

***Figure 3-29.*** *Agent training*

Click the UPLOAD button. Then click the Choose File button to upload the text file containing the conversation log, as shown in Figure 3-30.

💬 Upload logs file                                    BACK

You can upload user inputs to the Training tool in one .txt file (one line per phrase) or in .zip archive with multiple (up to 10) .txt files. A single .txt file or unpacked .zip archive should not exceed 3 MB.

[Choose File]   No file chosen

You can drag and drop the file here.

***Figure 3-30.*** *Uploading a file*

Once the file is successfully uploaded, then click the Back button to view the uploaded list of conversation logs, as shown in Figure 3-31. It shows the list of all the requests with the date, total number of requests, and number of requests that are not matched to an intent. For each request, the matched intent will be shown below the user query, as shown in Figure 3-31.

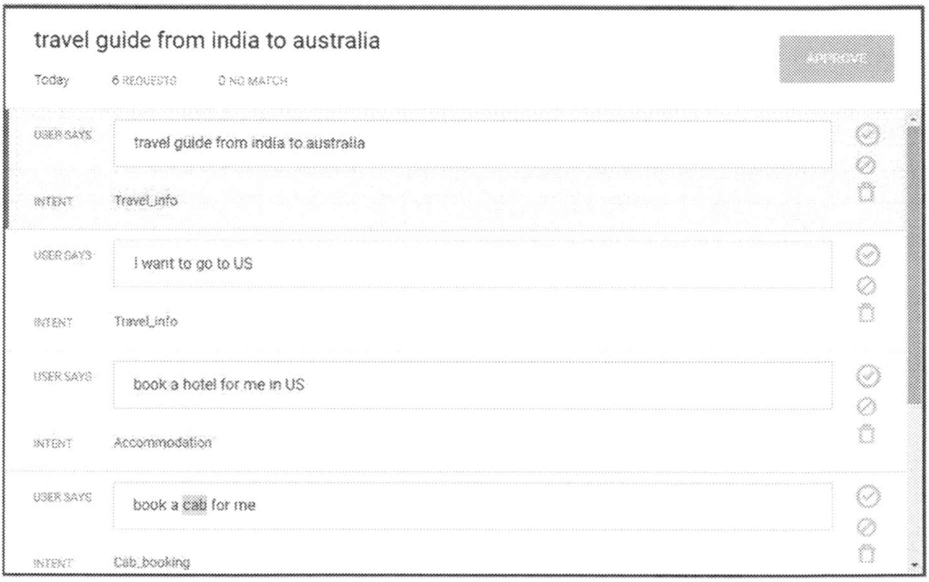

travel guide from india to australia                              APPROVE

Today      6 REQUESTS      0 NO MATCH

| USER SAYS | travel guide from india to australia |
| INTENT | Travel_info |

| USER SAYS | I want to go to US |
| INTENT | Travel_info |

| USER SAYS | book a hotel for me in US |
| INTENT | Accommodation |

| USER SAYS | book a cab for me |
| INTENT | Cab_booking |

***Figure 3-31.*** *Agent training*

For requests not matched to a specific intent, the default fallback intent will appear, as shown in Figure 3-32.

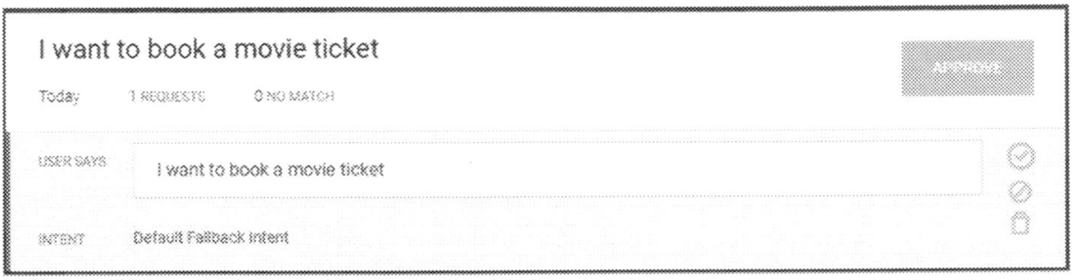

**Figure 3-32.** *Agent training*

For each request, you can choose to perform an action to improve your agent.

You can add the request to the currently matched intent by following these steps:

1. Click the check mark icon at the top right.

2. The check mark will turn green; click the Approve button to update the intent, as shown in Figure 3-33.

**Figure 3-33.** *Approving the intent*

The user can also add the request to a different intent.

Click the current intent name, and you will see the list of associated intents to the agent, as shown in Figure 3-34.

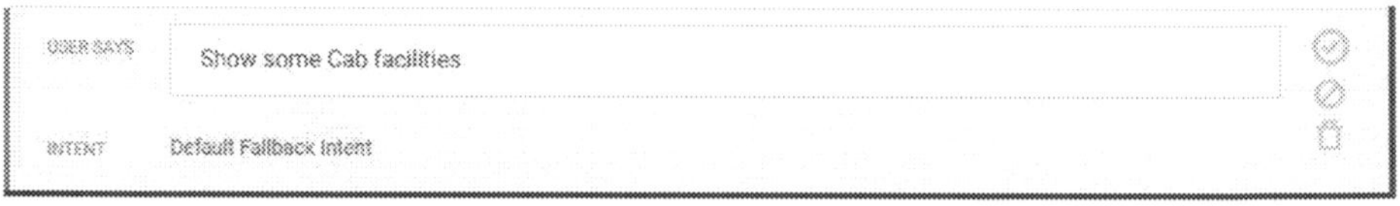

**Figure 3-34.** *Intent list*

Select the intent you want to add, as shown in Figure 3-35.

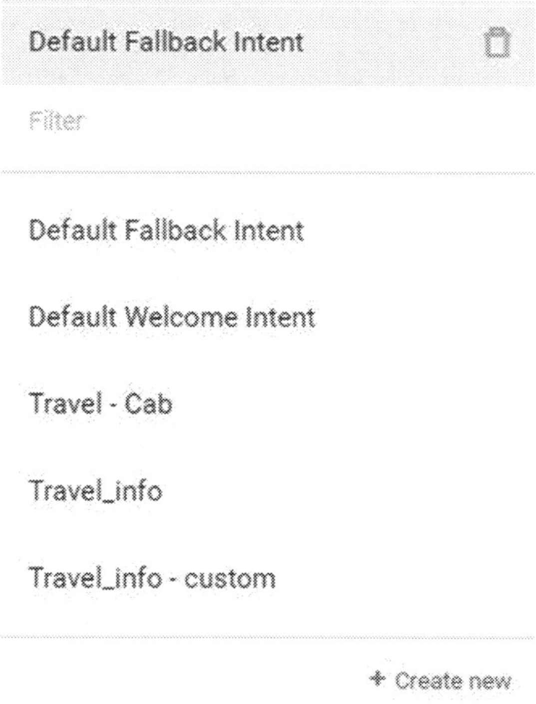

**Figure 3-35.** *Intent list*

The check mark icon changes to green; click the Approve button, as shown in Figure 3-36.

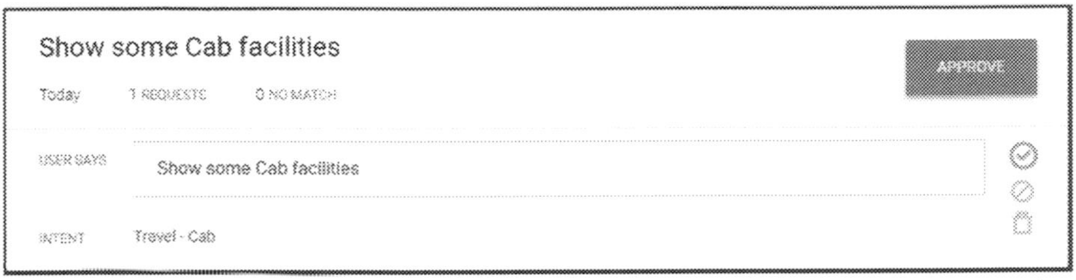

**Figure 3-36.** *Approving the intent*

After adding a request to an intent, you will see the selected intent, as shown in Figure 3-37.

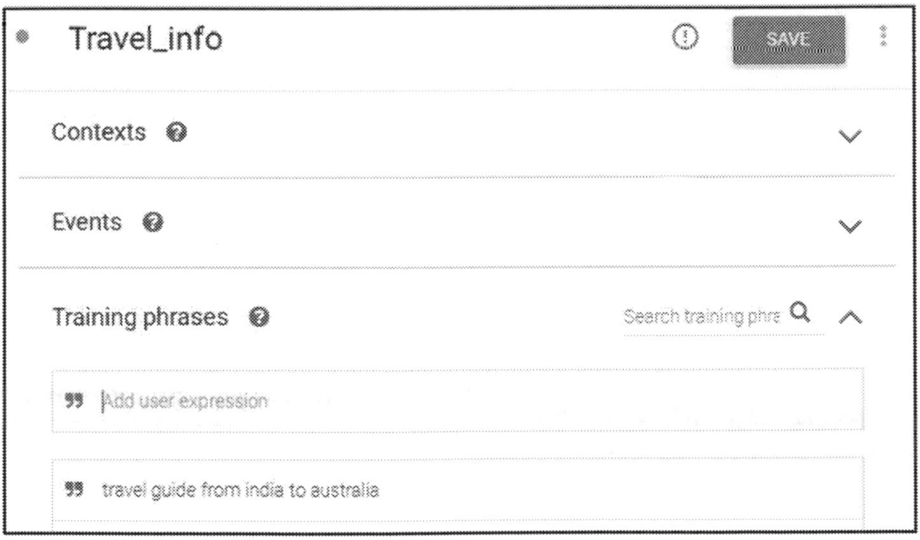

**Figure 3-37.** *Saving the intent*

# Agent Settings

We can apply various agent settings to an agent.

1. Go to the Google Dialogflow page.

2. Click the Settings button next to the agent in the left
   sidebar menu. This opens the agent's settings page,
   as shown in Figure 3-38.

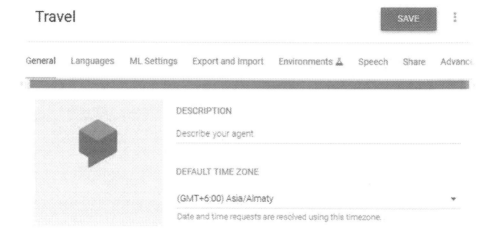

*Figure 3-38.*   *Agent settings*

Here is a breakdown of the settings:

**Description**: Give a description of your agent.

**Default Time Zone**: Select the time zone of your agent.

These are the options under Google Project:

- **Project ID**: This is the project ID of the Google Cloud
  Platform project linked to the agent, as shown in
  Figure 3-39.

- **Service Account**: This is the service account for
  authentication.

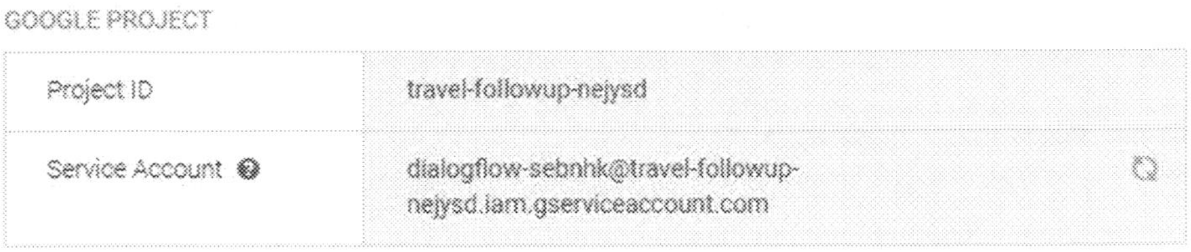

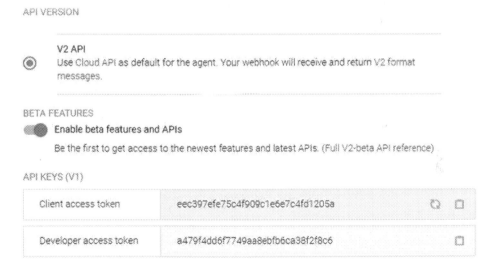

**Figure 3-39.** *Google Project settings*

One option appears under API Version:

- Select the API version the for agent, which here is V2 API, as shown in Figure 3-40.

**Figure 3-40.** *API Version setting*

One option appears under Beta Features:

- Turn the toggle button on/off to enable beta features for your agent.

These are the options under API Keys:

- **Client access token**: Generate a client access token.

- **Developer access token**: Generate a new key pair with the Refresh button.

These are the settings under Log Settings:

- **Log interactions to Dialogflow**: Toggle this button to enable/disable logging of user queries.

- **Log interactions to Google Cloud**: Toggle this button to enable/disable logging to Google Cloud. This option is not available if log interaction to Dialogflow is disabled.

These are the settings under Delete Agent:

- **Delete This Agent**: This completely deletes the agent and cannot be undone, as shown in Figure 3-41. Remove all the users before deleting the agent.

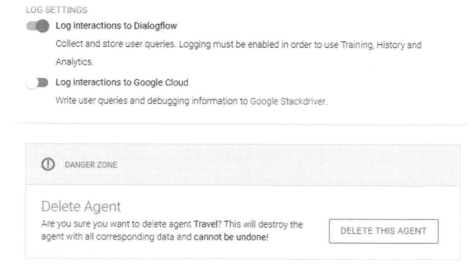

*Figure 3-41.*  *Deleting an agent*

These are the settings under Languages:

- The default language is set to English. You can add multiple languages.

- Click "+Add locale" to add a location (if available).

- Click Save after adding a language and locale, as shown in Figure 3-42.

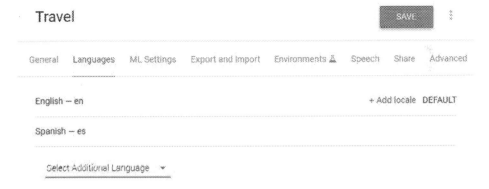

*Figure 3-42.* *Agent language*

Under ML Settings, choose one of the options according to the agent, as shown in Figure 3-43.

- **Hybrid (Rule-based and ML)**: This is for agents with a small number of examples/templates of intents.

- **ML only**: This is for agents with a large number of examples of intents.

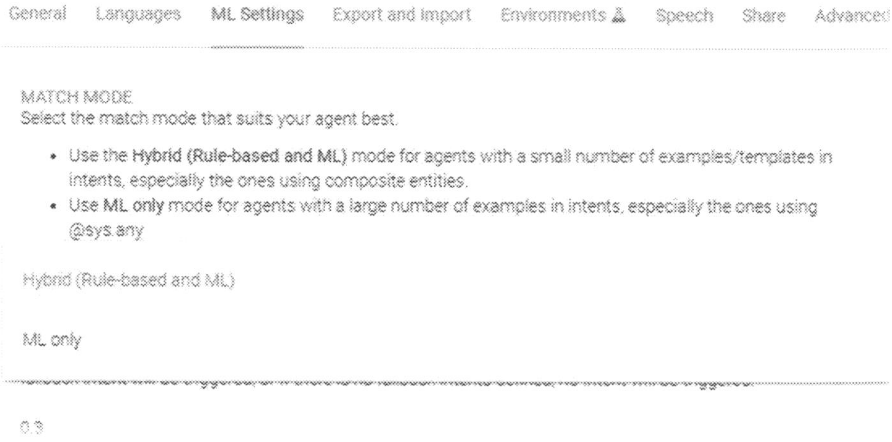

General    Languages    **ML Settings**    Export and Import    Environments ⚠    Speech    Share    Advanced

MATCH MODE
Select the match mode that suits your agent best.

- Use the **Hybrid (Rule-based and ML)** mode for agents with a small number of examples/templates in intents, especially the ones using composite entities.
- Use **ML only** mode for agents with a large number of examples in intents, especially the ones using @sys.any

Hybrid (Rule-based and ML)

ML only

03

*Figure 3-43.* *ML Settings options*

These are the spelling-related options:

- **Automatic Spell Correction**: Enable this to correct the spelling in queries, as shown in Figure 3-44.

- **Automatic Training**: Enable or disable automatic agent training each time the agent is modified, as shown in Figure 3-44.

- **Agent Validation**: Enable this to automatically validate the agent after performing agent training, as shown in Figure 3-44.

*Figure 3-44.* *Spell correction*

These are the options on the Export and Import tab:

- **Export as ZIP**: Exports the agent as a zip file, as shown
  in Figure 3-45.

- **Restore from ZIP**: Overwrites the current agent with
  the supplied zip file, as shown in Figure 3-45.

- **Import from ZIP**: Adds intents and entities to the
  current agent from the supplied zip file. If any existing
  intents or entities have the same name as those in the
  zip file, they will be replaced.

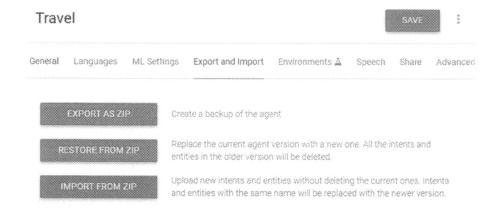

**Figure 3-45.**  *Exporting and importing*

On the Environments tab, you can publish and create versions of your agent for a specific environment, as shown in Figure 3-46. Multiple environments can be set up depending on your needs, like Development, Testing, and Production.

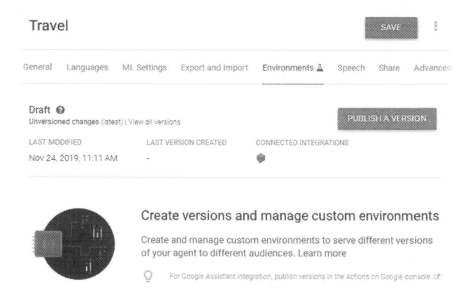

**Figure 3-46.**  *Environments tab*

These are the options under Improve Speech Recognition Quality:

- **Enable Enhanced Speech Models and Data Logging**: Toggle this button to enable enhanced speech models and logging, as shown in Figure 3-47.

- **Enable Auto Speech Adaptation**: Toggle this button to enable auto speech adaptation, as shown in Figure 3-47.

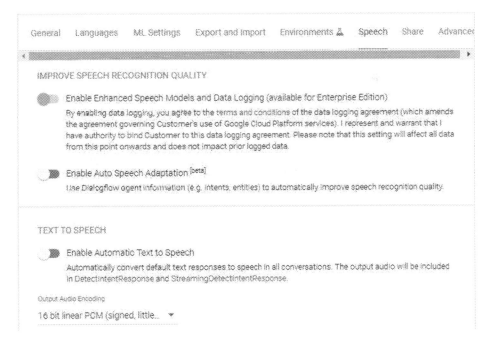

***Figure 3-47.*** *Speech configuration*

These are the text to speech options:

- **Enable Automatic Text to Speech**: Toggle this button to enable the automatic conversion of text to speech for every conversation, as shown in Figure 3-48.

- **Output audio encoding**: Select the encoding type (16-bit linear PCM, MP3, Ogg Opus).

- **Voice Configuration**: There are several options here:

    - **Agent Language**: Select the agent language.

    - **Voice:** Choose a voice synthesis model.

    - **Speaking Rate**: Adjust the voice speaking rate.

    - **Pitch**: Adjust the voice pitch.

    - **Volume Gain**: Adjust the audio volume gain.

    - **Audio Effects Profile**: Select the audio effects
      profiles that you want applied to the synthesized
      voice.

- **Experiment with Different Voice Setting**: Type some
  text and hit Play to test different voice settings.

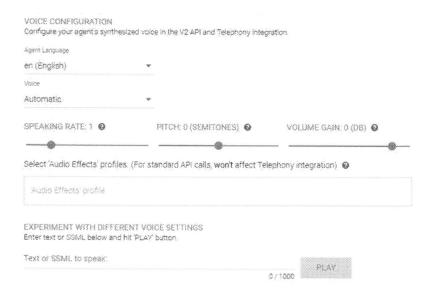

***Figure 3-48.*** *Agent voice configuration*

On the Share tab, you can send an invite to new people to share and
grant access to your agent, as shown in Figure 3-49.

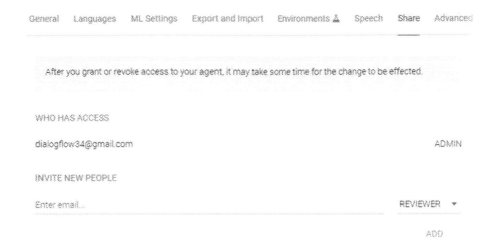

*Figure 3-49.* *Agent access configuration*

On the Advanced tab, under Sentiment Analysis, toggle this button to enable sentiment analysis and provide a sentiment score for each user query, as shown in Figure 3-50.

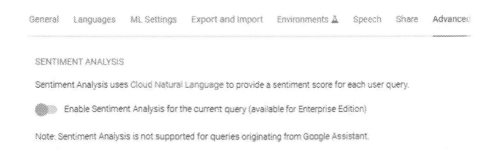

*Figure 3-50.* *Agent advanced features*

# Multilingual Chatbots

Consider a scenario where you need to build a chatbot for an organization whose users are spread across different geographic locations and converse in different languages. How would you build a conversation system that can handle such diversity?

There are multiple solutions that can be used.

- Build a base conversation system in the English language, in other words, with the intent and entity configuration in the English language and the responses defined in different languages. However, sometimes this solution may fail to capture some language-specific context that is essential for building good conversation systems.

- Build a single conversation agent and define the configuration (i.e., intents, entities, parameters, and responses) specific to the language.

The preferred approach is to build an end-to-end system in multiple languages for higher accuracy. In this scenario, we need to provide training phrases for intent classification, entity variations, and parameter prompts if required in the target language. This is how Google Dialogflow implements a multilingual conversation system.

You can download the agent that has the use case configured for the travel domain in different languages.

Go to `https://github.com/dialogflow34/Chat-Bot/tree/master/Chapter_3` to download the `Travel_multilingual.zip` file.

Import the downloaded agent into Google Dialogflow, as explained in Chapter 2.

Go to the top-left menu and click the + sign next to the default language (i.e., en), as shown in Figure 3-51. This will open the Language tab on the agent's settings page. Set the language to French and click the Save button to save the changes, as shown in Figure 3-52.

*Figure 3-51.*  *Agent configuration*

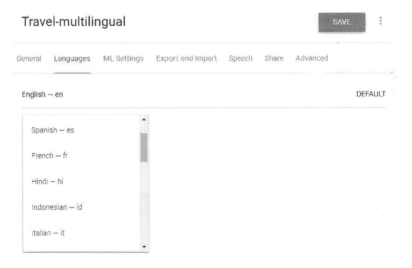

*Figure 3-52.*  *Language configuration*

Now, a new language, i.e., French, has been added to your agent. Next, you need to configure both intents (i.e., Travel_info and Travel_Cab) with the training phrases in French, as shown in Figure 3-53.

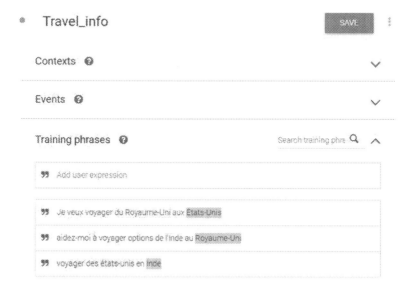

***Figure 3-53.*** *Multilingual chatbot, training phrases*

Next, define the prompt text for parameters in French only, as shown in Figure 3-54. Also, change the response in the Responses section to French, as shown in Figure 3-55.

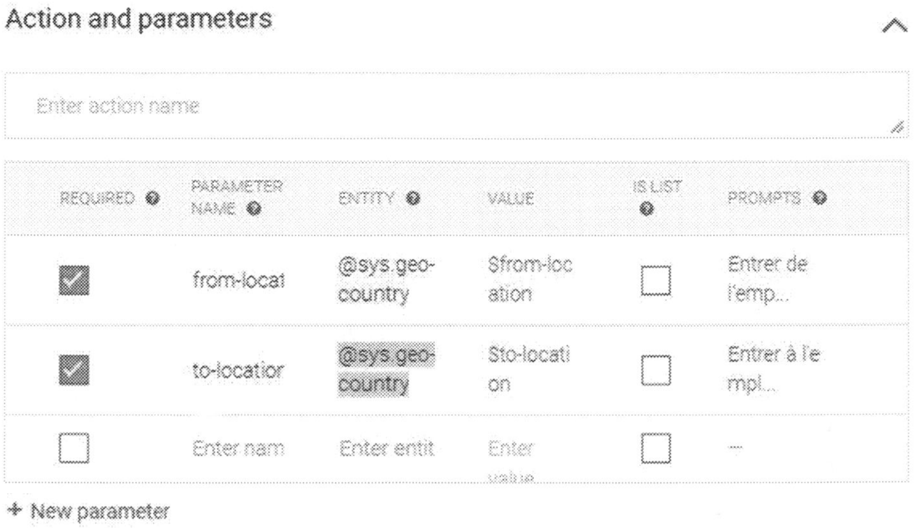

**Figure 3-54.** *Multilingual chatbot, "Action and parameters" page*

**Figure 3-55.** *Multilingual chatbot, response*

Now, go to Integrations, open the Web Demo URL, and enter the query
**Je veux voyager des États-Unis au Royaume-Uni**, which is the French
translation of *I want to travel from US to UK*. The agent recognizes the
intent as Travel_info for this query and responds accordingly, as shown in
Figure 3-56.

*Figure 3-56.* *Multilingual chatbot, Web Demo*

# Prebuilt Agents

Prebuilt agents are agents trained on common topics such as weather,
traffic, unit conversion, and so on. These agents have a predefined set of
intents along with training phrases, entities, and parameters. So, if you
want to leverage use cases related to these common topics, then you can
use them in a new agent or copy them into an existing agent.

As a continuation of our travel use case, if the user is also looking for the weather conditions of the location where he is planning to travel, then we can use prebuilt agents to configure this in our existing agent. We will start with the configuration of a prebuilt agent, which will create a new agent by default, and then we will move intents from this newly created agent to the existing one.

Go to the left menu bar and click Prebuilt Agents. Select the Weather prebuilt agent, and click the IMPORT button, as shown in Figure 3-57.

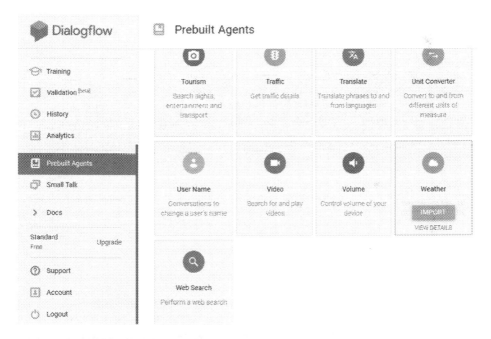

***Figure 3-57.*** *Prebuilt agents*

You can also click the VIEW DETAILS link just below the IMPORT button to see some of the sample user utterances that have been configured in some of the intents of the Weather agent, as shown in Figure 3-58.

***Figure 3-58.***  *Example intents of prebuilt Weather agent*

Wait for a few seconds, and Dialogflow will create a new agent with the name Weather, as shown in Figure 3-59.

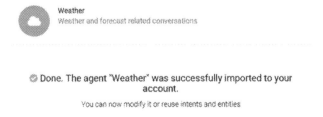

***Figure 3-59.***  *New agent created, based on prebuilt Weather agent*

Now, a new agent with the name Weather has been added to our account. To check, click the drop-down menu next to the current agent name (i.e., Travel) and click the "View all agents" link, as shown in Figure 3-60.

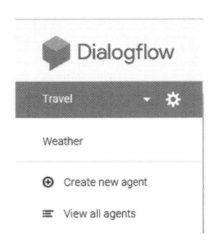

***Figure 3-60.*** *"View all agents" link*

This will show a list of the available agents to our account where we can see the Weather agent listed, as shown in Figure 3-61.

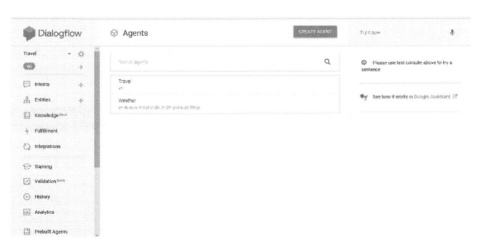

***Figure 3-61.*** *List of agents*

You can also see a list of preconfigured intents listed under the Weather agent by clicking the Intents tab in the left menu bar, as shown in Figure 3-62.

Next, if you want to see list of available intents and their training phrases, then do the following:

1. Go to the left menu bar and click the drop-down menu next to the agent name and select the Weather agent.

2. Go to the left menu bar and click the Intents option. This will populate a list of available intents under an agent named Weather, as shown in Figure 3-62.

***Figure 3-62.*** *Weather agent's Intents list*

We can also see training phrases, contexts, and entities for each of intents corresponding to the Weather agent. For example, click one of intents (i.e., *weather)* for the Weather agent. This will populate details such as training phrases, contexts, entities, etc., for the intent called *weather*, as shown in Figure 3-63.

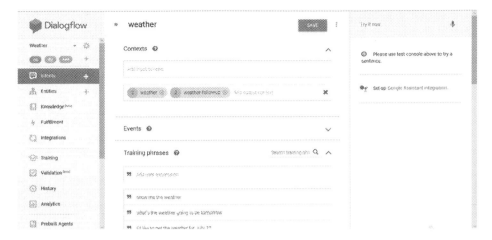

**Figure 3-63.** *Weather intent configuration*

The Weather agent populates some default parameters as part of the weather intent. But for now, we have removed all parameters as we just wanted to show the integration to our Travel agent. We will discuss the parameters for the weather intent in the next section.

Since we want our chatbot to be able to answer weather-related questions, we will copy the weather intent from the Weather agent to our Travel agent to answer weather-related queries for a city. Select the weather intent to open up a menu on top with the options such as COPY, MOVE, DELETE, and CANCEL. Click the COPY button, as shown in Figure 3-64.

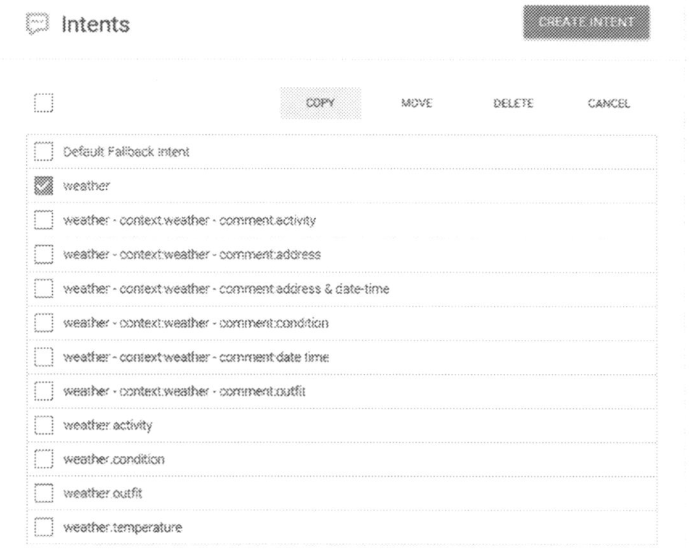

**Figure 3-64.** *Prebuilt agent, copying the intent*

Next, it will ask for the target agent. Select Travel [en] as your target agent and select the check box "Copy related entities." Once done, click the Start button, as shown in Figure 3-65.

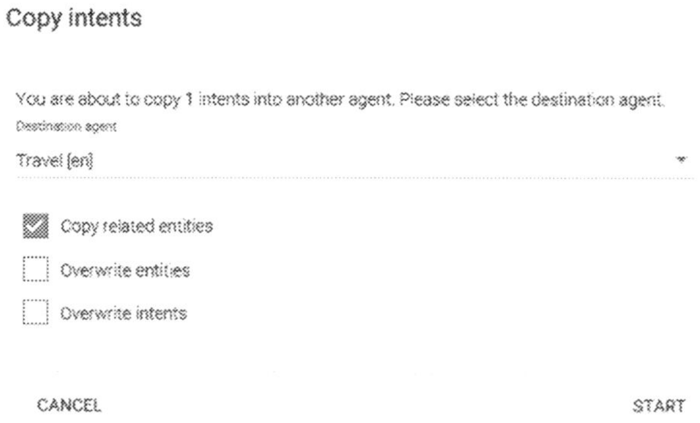

**Figure 3-65.** *Copying the intent to the Travel agent*

This will then add the weather intent along with its associated entities to our Travel agent. After a successful transfer, click the PROCEED TO AGENT button to see a list of intents in our Travel agent, as shown in Figure 3-66.

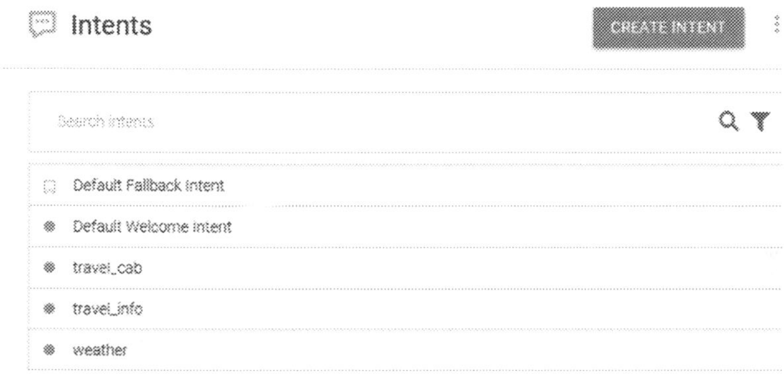

*Figure 3-66.*  *Intents list*

Now, the weather intent has been added to our Travel agent. So, users can ask questions related to the weather conditions. Go to the "Try it out" panel and enter the query shown in Figure 3-67.

In Figure 3-67, our Travel agent is able to categorize the query (i.e., *Show me weather*) into the weather intent.

In this section, we have copied the weather intent and entities from an existing Weather agent. Our Travel agent is now able to analyze weather-related questions. In the next section, we will discuss fulfillment and webhooks, which can be used to integrate with the Weather API to fetch weather information.

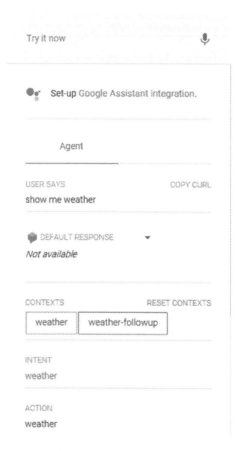

***Figure 3-67.*** *Trying out the weather intent*

# Fulfillment: Integration with the Weather API

Up until now, we have integrated the weather intent and related entities from the prebuilt Weather agent to our Travel agent. Next, we will discuss how our webhook service can be used to integrate Dialogflow and the Weather API.

Before that, we will deep dive into some basic concepts such as fulfillment, webhook services, and third-party APIs, as shown in Figure 3-68.

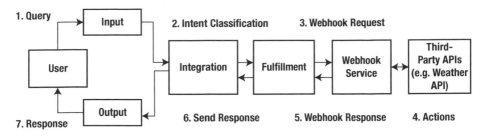

***Figure 3-68.*** *Integration of Weather API with Dialogflow*

# Fulfillment

Fulfillment helps to integrate your service with the agent to populate dynamic responses to end users. For example, if you want to check the weather conditions in a city, then your chatbot response should be changed as per the weather conditions of the respective city.

# Webhook Service

Since Dialogflow can't directly integrate with any third-party API, it is only possible via your service that facilitates communication between Dialogflow and third-party APIs. Webhook services perform this task. You can write webhook services in any programming language of your choice and release them as REST APIs. Please make sure your webhook service is publicly accessible and accepts only POST requests. You can deploy your webhook service either in the virtual machine or in compute functions in any cloud provider. You can download the sample code that has the use case configured for weather integration.

Go to `https://github.com/dialogflow34/Chat-Bot/tree/master/Chapter_3` to download the `Travel_Weather_code.txt` file.

# Open Source Weather API

Go to the following link to get an open source weather API:

`https://home.openweathermap.org/`

You will be redirected to the page shown in Figure 3-69. Click the sign-up button to create an account.

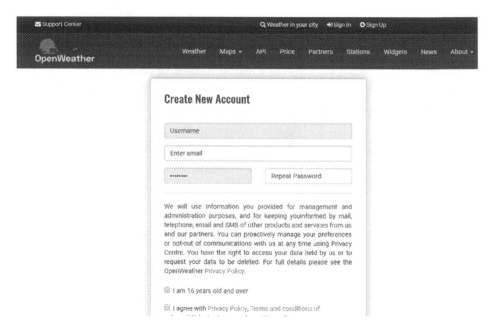

***Figure 3-69.***  *Sign-up page*

Fill in the required details to create an account, as shown in Figure 3-70.

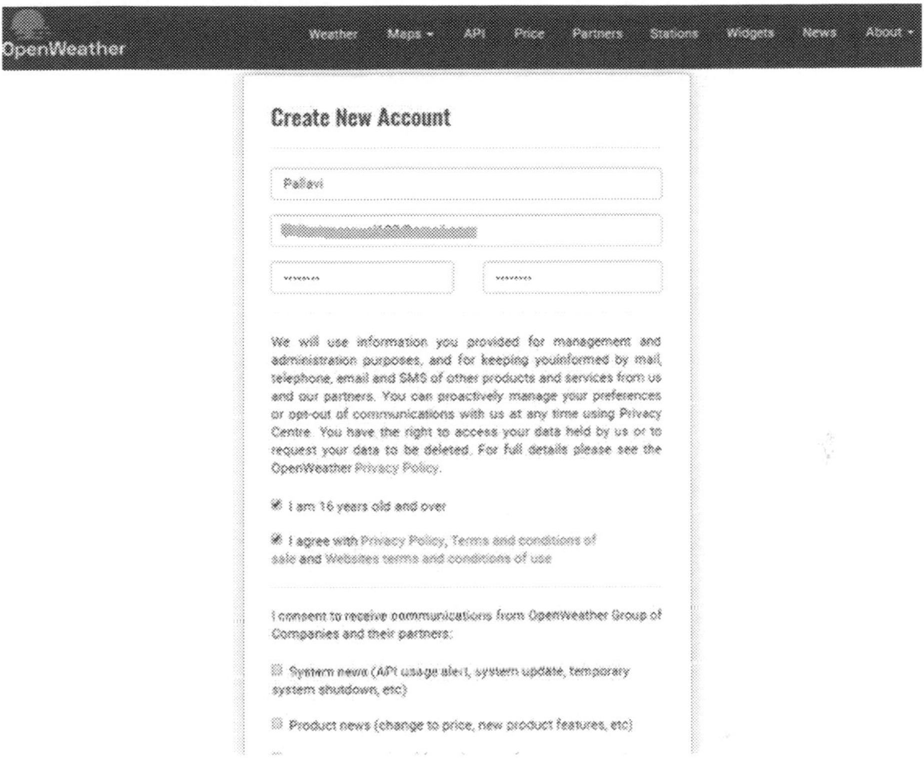

*Figure 3-70.*  *Sign-up page filled in*

A confirmation e-mail with your API key and technical instructions will be sent to your registered e-mail address. Please note that it takes up to two hours to activate the API key, as shown in Figure 3-71.

> **Thank you for subscribing to OpenWeather API!**
>
> Dear Customer!
>
> Thank you for subscribing to Free OpenWeather API!
>
> API key:
> - Your API key is **38005ca4a5a7a2842bdde708bbc93da7**
> - Within the next couple of hours, it will be activated and ready to use
> - You can later create more API keys on your account page
> - Please, always use your API key in each API call
>
> Endpoint:
> - Please, use the endpoint api.openweathermap.org for your API calls
> - Example of API call:
> api.openweathermap.org/data/2.5/weather?q=London,uk&APPID=
> 38005ca4a5a7a2842bdde708bbc93da7
>
> Useful links:
> - API documentation https://openweathermap.org/api
> - Details of your plan https://openweathermap.org/price
> - Please, note that 16-days daily forecast and History API are not available for Free subscribers
>
>
> Blog
> Support center & FAQ
> Contact us info@openweathermap.org.

***Figure 3-71.***  *E-mail verification page*

As the next step, go to the API tab to check the freely available weather API document.

Check this API URL through a browser as well. It will show the weather forecast details, as shown in Figure 3-72.

In this case, we are using the URL to call the API with the city name: `http://api.openweathermap.org/data/2.5/weather?q=DELHI&units=me` `tric&APPID=19e8588cb3d7d0623e3a5a8ec529232f.`

*Figure 3-72.* *Showing API result in a browser*

In this section, we will showcase the integration of the Weather API to Google Dialogflow.

The complete scenario works as follows:

1. Dialogflow calls the webhook service via fulfillment with the required input.

2. The webhook service processes an input request from Dialogflow and sends it to the Weather API.

3. The Weather API processes requests from the webhook and returns a response to the webhook service.

4. The webhook service converts a response from the Weather API to a format that Dialogflow can understand and send it to Dialogflow via fulfillment for further processing.

You can download the agent that has the use case configured for weather.

Go to `https://github.com/dialogflow34/Chat-Bot/tree/master/Chapter_3` to download the `Travel_weather.zip` file.

Import the downloaded agent into Google Dialogflow, as explained in Chapter 2.

We will proceed with the weather intent that was configured in the previous section where we will integrate Dialogflow with the Weather API using fulfillment via a webhook service. For this book, we have created a webhook service in the Python programming language with a sample request and response JSON.

Here is the input JSON:

```json
{
  "responseId": "12c5e0ed-7ec3-4ce6-938e-ce1a5fa5ceaf-
  7e4f1f27",
  "queryResult": {
    "queryText": "show me weather in London",
    "parameters": {
      "geo-city": "London"
    },
    "allRequiredParamsPresent": true,
    "intent": {
      "name": "projects/weather-hvucqi/agent/intents/9965f638-
      213e-4f1d-82a0-9928013f707c",
      "displayName": "Weather"
    },
    "intentDetectionConfidence": 1,
    "languageCode": "en"
  },
  "originalDetectIntentRequest": {
    "payload": {}
  },
  "session": "projects/weather-hvucqi/agent/sessions/67c6b15b-
  6cbc-a495-8bdd-50bd023f0eb7"
}
```

Here is the output JSON:

```json
{

    "fulfillmentText": "Weather Report of London --> Current
    Temperature : 11.82, Pressure : 1003, Humidity : 93, temp_
    min : 10.56, temp_max : 13.33",
    "fulfillmentMessages": [
```

```
{
    "text": {
        "text": [
            "Weather Report of London --> Current
            Temperature : 11.82, Pressure : 1003,
            Humidity : 93, temp_min : 10.56, temp_max :
            13.33"
        ]
    }
}
],
"source": "weather-webhook"
}
```

Next, we will add one mandatory parameter to the weather intent (i.e., geo-city), which will store entries of entity @sys.geo-city to value @geo-city if that is being recognized from the user input. Since this is a mandatory parameter, it will keep asking prompt questions to the user until this parameter has been provided (slot filling), as shown in Figure 3-73.

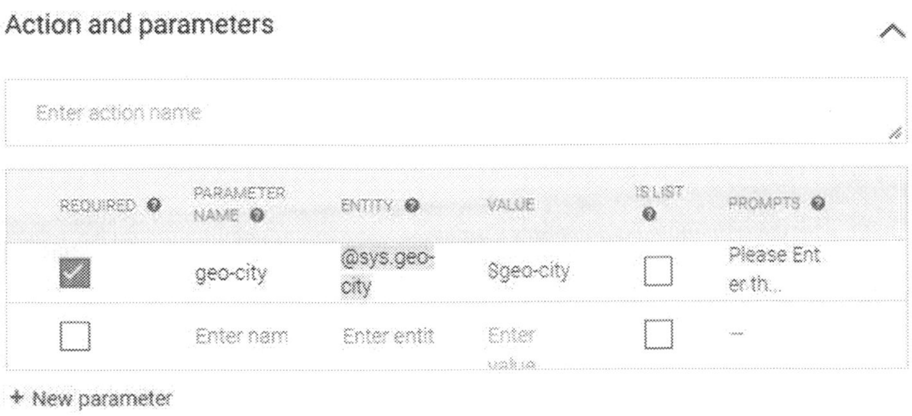

**Action and parameters**

| REQUIRED | PARAMETER NAME | ENTITY | VALUE | IS LIST | PROMPTS |
|---|---|---|---|---|---|
| ☑ | geo-city | @sys.geo-city | $geo-city | ☐ | Please Ent er th... |
| ☐ | Enter nam | Enter entit | Enter value | ☐ | ... |

+ New parameter

***Figure 3-73.*** *Configuring a parameter*

Now, go to the Fulfillment section under the weather intent and click the drop-down menu. Toggle the "Enable webhook call for this intent" option, as shown in Figure 3-74. This will enable webhook calling for this intent. Here, your web service will be called as soon as the weather intent has been recognized and all slots have been filled.

***Figure 3-74.***  *Enabling the webhook call*

Go to the top-left menu and click Fulfillment. This will open a new page where either you can call your webhook service or use an inline editor to call the Weather API. For this book, we will call the webhook service. Click the toggle button on the right side of the Webhook label, as shown in Figure 3-75.

***Figure 3-75.***  *Enabling fulfillment*

We have used ngrok to enable our webhook service to be accessible publicly. Once enabled, provide the URL, username, and password if required. For now, our webhook service doesn't require any username and password, but all communication with the webhook service is encrypted. Click the Save button to configure fulfillment for this webhook service, as shown in Figure 3-76.

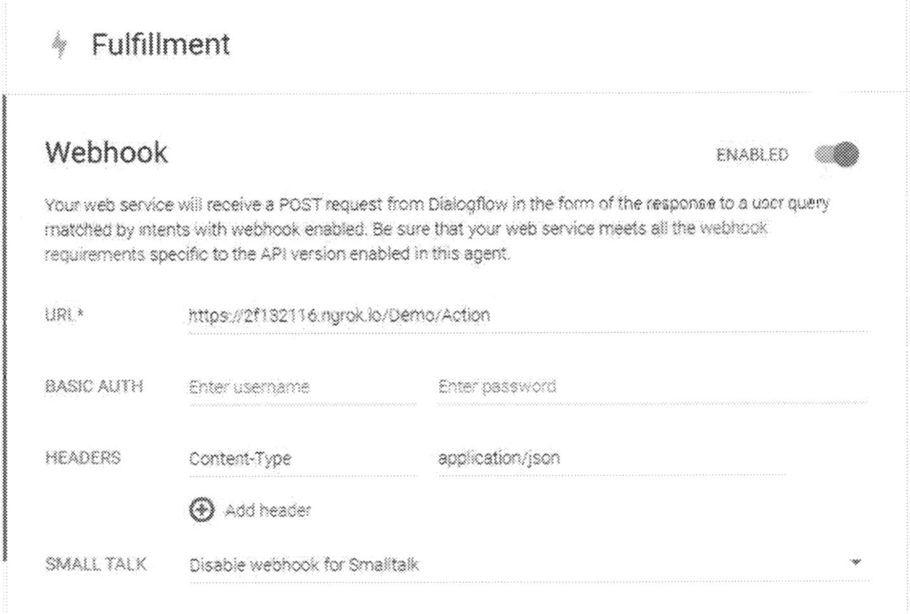

*Figure 3-76.* *Configuring fulfillment*

Now, go to the left menu and click the Integrations tab. Enable Web Demo integration and open the Web Demo URL in a browser of your choice. Next, the user can start a conversation with our Travel agent, as shown in Figure 3-77.

**Figure 3-77.**  *Web Demo, weather intent identification*

After classification of the user's query to the weather intent, it asks for a location as this is a mandatory parameter that needs to be provided. Once the intent has been recognized and the slot has been filled, then it will call your webhook service with these arguments. Your webhook service calls the Weather API to fetch the weather information for the selected city and sends a response to the webhook service, which provides the response in a Dialogflow-specific format to Dialogflow, as shown in Figure 3-78.

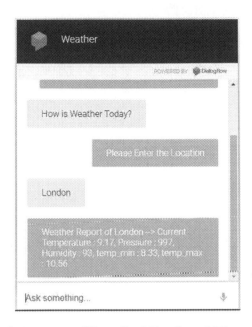

***Figure 3-78.*** *Web Demo, calling the Weather API*

# Conclusion

In this chapter, we discussed how to design a complex use case using the concepts of input and output contexts, follow-up intents, etc. This chapter also explained various use cases with multiple intents, enabling fulfillment, and using webhooks for integration with external APIs to further enrich the quality of the conversation in our agent. We also explained how prebuilt agents can be used to reduce the time required to configure an agent for out-of-the-box use cases.

# CHAPTER 4

# Chatbot Enrichment

In this chapter, we will describe some advanced use cases that leverage the capabilities of Google Dialogflow. We have already discussed fulfillment and using the webhook service to integrate with third-party APIs, so in this chapter we will focus on chatbot personality, sentiment analysis, events, and integration with third-party messengers such as Facebook. We will also look at the Google knowledge base and implement a document search feature in Google Dialogflow.

## Chatbot Personality

A chatbot's *personality* can be defined as the human-like qualities it exhibits in its conversations with end users. When building a chatbot for an organization, the chatbot's personality represents an important element; otherwise, the chatbot will converse in a robot-like fashion with no emotions. For personality, we can use traits such as being friendly, formal, helpful, or polite in conversations with end users.

There are various ways to implement chatbot personality. Some organizations build their own organization-specific personality, and others implement common personality questions.

© Navin Sabharwal, Amit Agrawal 2020
N. Sabharwal and A. Agrawal, *Cognitive Virtual Assistants Using Google Dialogflow*,
https://doi.org/10.1007/978-1-4842-5741-8_4

Here, we have collected some general personality questions along with their answers and have built a natural language processing–based retrieval model that returns the relevant answers to personality questions asked by the user. For example:

- *What are you doing?*

- *What is your name?*

For this book, we have developed our own personality module in the Python language. For this exercise, you can go to `https://github.com/dialogflow34/Chat-Bot/tree/master/Chapter_4` to download the code.

Download and unzip the folder `Personality_Code.zip`. This folder contains five subfolders/packages.

- **config**: Contains all the configuration files for the code

- **data**: Contains all the data files such as training data or model files

- **logs**: Contains all the log files

- **models**: Contains the Python code files for various models used in this code

- **utils**: Contains the Python code files for various natural language processing (NLP) tasks

Please refer to the Python code file `corpus.py` inside the `model` package. This Python code file has a Python class that implements various functions to train and use a personality model for a user's query, as discussed in this chapter.

We will start by importing all of the necessary predefined and user-defined packages, as shown here:

```
import sys
import os

cmd_new = '.'
import csv
import utils
from utils import nlpTask as nlp
from utils import fileOperations as fileOp
from utils import mongoDBOperations as mongo
import logging
import ConfigParser
import os
from config import *
import pandas as pd
import jaccard_index as jaccard
import time
from ConfigParser import SafeConfigParser
import os
```

Next, we will define the Python class PersonalityModel with the required variables, as shown here:

```
class PersonalityModel:
    fieldMaps = {}
    fieldNames=['question_text', 'question_tokens', 'answer']
    modelDirectory = "
    modelFileNames = {}
    categoryMaps = {}
    corpusMaps = {}
    questionKeys = {}
    categoryDataFrame = pd.DataFrame()
```

```
    fieldDataFrame = pd.DataFrame()
    questionDict = {}
    answerDict = {}
    questionList = []
    questionTokenList = []
    answerList = []
    vocab = []

    vocabFileName = \
config.get('COMMONFILES', 'VOCAB_FILENAME')
```

Now, we will discuss how to train the personality module, as shown in the following function:

```
@staticmethod
    def buildGenericModel(customerName):
        try:
            collectionName = 'Common'
            PersonalityModel.modelDirectory = \
 cmd_new + '/data/' + customerName
            logger.info('Creating directory for customer {0} \
            with name {1}'.format(customerName, \
                              PersonalityModel.modelDirectory))
            If not \
            os.path.exists(PersonalityModel.modelDirectory):
                os.makedirs(PersonalityModel.modelDirectory)
            PersonalityModel.categoryDataFrame = \
mongo.getDocumentContent(customerName, ['category'])
            data = \
            mongo.getDocumentContent(collectionName, ['category'])
            categoryList = \
            list(set(list(PersonalityModel.categoryDataFrame
            ['category'])))
```

```
        for category in categoryList:
            PersonalityModel.fieldDataFrame = \
            mongo.getDocumentContent(customerName, \
            PersonalityModel.fieldNames)
            PersonalityModel.modelFileNames[ \
                category] = \
PersonalityModel.modelDirectory + '/' + customerName + '_' +
category + '_model.pkl'
            PersonalityModel.fieldDataFrame.to_
pickle(PersonalityModel.modelFileNames[category])
            PersonalityModel.loadModel(customerName, category)

    except Exception, e:
        logger.error('Exception occured while \
        creating generic model')
        logger.error('Exception details......%s',  e)
```

In this function, we are loading training data from the MongoDB database and storing it in a pickle file that will be used to recommend a relevant answer for a user's query.

The following code snippets will show you how to use this pickle file and model to recommend a relevant answer to the user's query. The function getRecommendation receives the following arguments as parameters:

- **customerName**: This is used to distinguish between multiple implementations across customers. Possible values are HCL and IBM.

- **inputQuery**: This is the user's query (for example, *What is your name?*).

This returns the JSON variable jsonResponse that contains an answer to the query. As an example, for the *What is your name?* query, jsonResponse contains the following answer: *Hey! I am chatbot.*

*What about you?*. The definition of this function starts with the declaration of the required Python variables, as shown here:

```
def getRecommendation(self, customerName, inputQuery):
        try:
                jsonResponse = {}
                stemWords = []
                responseDict = {}
                responseList = []
                spellList = []
                category = 'Greetings'
                model_category = 'Common'
```

Next, we will check whether the trained model is already available in memory. Load the model if it is not available, as shown here:

```
                if \
                PersonalityModel.fieldDataFrame.empty:
                        self.loadModel(model_category, category)
```

Now, we perform NLP tasks such as tokenization, stemming, spell correction, etc., on `inputQuery`, as shown here:

```
                processQuery = \
                nlp.extract_word(nlp.punct_tokenize(inputQuery))
                spellList = \
                nlp.spell_checker(processQuery, PersonalityModel.
                vocab)
                processQuery = nlp.word_stem(spellList)
```

These NLP tasks and related code snippets are available in the Python code file `nlpTask.py` inside the `utils` package. The definitions of all of these functions are as follows:

*Function: punct_tokenize*

```
def punct_tokenize(summary):
    try:
        return \
wordpunct_tokenize(summary.lower().decode('utf-8', 'ignore'))
    except Exception, e:
        logger.error('Exception Occurred.......')
        logger.error('Exception Details.......%s', e)
```

*Function: extract_word*

```
def extract_word(tokens):
    try:
        filteredWords = []
        for token in tokens:
            if re.search('^[a-zA-Z]+$', token): \
                filteredWords.append(token)
        return filteredWords
    except Exception, e:
        logger.error('Exception Occurred.......')
        logger.error('Exception Details.......%s', e)
```

*Function: word_stem*

```
def word_stem(tokenList):
    try:
        # print tokenList
        stemmer = SnowballStemmer('english')
        stemmedTokens = [stemmer.stem(token) for token in
\ tokenList]
        # print stemmedTokens
        return stemmedTokens
```

```
    except Exception, e:
        logger.error('Exception Occurred.......')
        logger.error('Exception Details.......%s', e)
```

*Function: spell_checker*

```
def spell_checker(sentence, vocabulary=None):
    try:
        logger.info('validating sentence {} against spell
\   checker'.format(sentence))
        spell_sentence = []
        sentence_stop = []
        spell_sentence_vocab = []
        lemma_sentence = []
        stop_correct_word = ' '
        vocab_correct_word = ' '
        stop_correct_word_score = 0
        vocab_correct_word_score = 0
        stopwords = set(nltk.corpus.stopwords.words('english') + \
        list(punctuation))
        for token in sentence:
            stop_correct_word, stop_correct_score = \
            similar_word(token, stopwords)
            vocab_correct_word, vocab_correct_score = \
            similar_word(token, vocabulary)
            if vocab_correct_word_score >= \
            stop_correct_word_score:
                spell_sentence.append(vocab_correct_word)
            else:
                spell_sentence.append(stop_correct_word)
        logger.info('correctly spelled sentence {0} for \
        actual sentence {1}'.format(spell_sentence, sentence))
```

```
        return spell_sentence

    except Exception, e:
        logger.error('Exception Occurred..........')
        logger.error('Exception details...........%s', e)
```

Next, we call the function find_similar_response to find the relevant answer to the query and generate the response JSON (i.e., jsonResponse), as shown here:

```
        responses = \
jaccard.find_similar_response(self.questionList, self.
questionTokenList, self.answerDict, \

self.questionDict, processQuery)
        jsonResponse['query'] = inputQuery
        jsonResponse['customer_name'] = customerName
        for response in responses:
            responseDict['response'] = response[1]
            responseDict['confidence'] = response[2]
            responseList.append(responseDict)
            responseDict = {}
        jsonResponse['responses'] = responseList

        return jsonResponse

    except Exception, e:
        logger.error('Exception occured while getting
recommendation for query %s for customer %s', inputQuery,
                    customerName)
        logger.error('Exception Details.......%s', e)
```

The find_similar_response function is defined in the Python code file jaccard_index.py inside the model package, as shown here:

```python
def find_similar_response(questionList, questionTokenList, \
answerDict, questionDict, question):
    similarity = []
    summary_list = []
    similarity = {}
    result_tuple = []
    # print questionTokenList
    try:
        for variation in questionList:
            similarity[variation] = compare(question, \
questionDict[variation])
        result = sorted(similarity.items(), \
        key=operator.itemgetter(1), reverse=True)[:5]
        if result[0][1] > 0.70:
            result_tuple.append((question, \
            random.choice(answerDict[result[0][0]]), \
            result[0][1]))

        else:
            if result[0][1] == 0:
                result_tuple.append((question, \
                config.get('RESPONSES', 'NO_RESULT'), \
                result[0][1]))
            else:
                similarity = {}
                questionResponse = {}
                for resultIndex in range(len(result)):
                    keys = similarity.keys()
                    max_score = 0.0
```

```
            response = \
            random.choice(answerDict[result[resultIndex]
            [0]])
            question = result[resultIndex][0]
            score = result[resultIndex][1]
            if response not in keys:
                similarity[response] = score
                questionResponse[question] = score
            else:
                if score > max_score:
                    similarity[response] = score
                    questionResponse[question] =   score
                    max_score = score
        similarity = sorted(similarity.items(), \
        key=operator.itemgetter(1), reverse=True)
        questionResponse = \
        sorted(questionResponse.items(), key=operator.
        itemgetter(1), reverse=True)
        print "dictionary", questionResponse
        for result in similarity:
            result_tuple.append((question, result[0], \
            result[1]))

    similarity = {}
    summary_list = []
    return result_tuple

except Exception, e:
    unique_logger.error('Exception Occured.........')
    unique_logger.error('Exception Details........%s', e)
```

This code snippet compares the processed form of the user's query with questions available as the part of training data and then returns an answer to a similar question as a response to the query.

So far, we have discussed how to train the personality module and use the trained model to find an answer to a question. Next, we will see how this system can be released as a REST API that can be consumed by other applications and software.

We will expose the personality module as a local URL. Since Google Dialogflow requires the public URL of your webhook service, we have used Ngrok to generate a public URL corresponding to our local URL.

Let's look at the steps to set up a personality webhook service on both Windows and Linux Server.

# Windows Server

For Windows Server, Python 3.6.x and PIP need to be installed in your system before continuing.

## Step 1: Install Flask-RESTful

Flask-RESTful is an extension of the microframework Flask for building REST APIs.

To install it, run the following command at the Windows command prompt, as shown in Figure 4-1:

```
pip install flask-restful
```

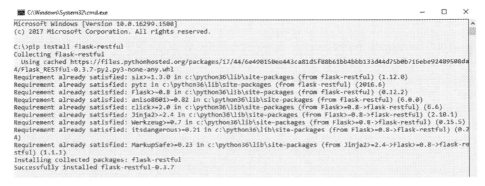

***Figure 4-1.*** *Windows command prompt showing installation of Flask-RESTful*

This will install the package and its dependencies.

## Step 2: Build the REST API

A RESTful API uses HTTP requests to get and post data.

Look for the PersonalityService.py file, which has code to release the personality module as a REST API, as shown here:

```python
import json
from flask import request
from flask_classful import FlaskView, route
from models.corpus import PersonalityModel

class EndPointCall(FlaskView):
    @route("/personality", methods=['POST'])
    def endpoint(self):

        personalityModel = PersonalityModel('testData')
        json_data = request.get_json(force=True)
        question = json_data["queryResult"]["queryText"]

        answer = \
        personalityModel.getRecommendation("testData",
        question)
        output = {
            "fulfillmentText": answer,
            "fulfillmentMessages": [{"text": {
                "text": [
                    answer
                ]
            }}],
            "source": "personality-webhook"
        }
        return json.dumps(output)
```

## Step 3: Deploy the Flask REST API

To deploy the REST API service using Flask, run the following command at the Window command prompt, as shown in Figure 4-2:

```
python PersonalityService.py
```

```
C:\Windows\System32\cmd.exe - python PersonalityService.py
Microsoft Windows [Version 10.0.16299.1508]
(c) 2017 Microsoft Corporation. All rights reserved.

C:\>python PersonalityService.py
 * Running on http://127.0.0.1:5000/ (Press CTRL+C to quit)
```

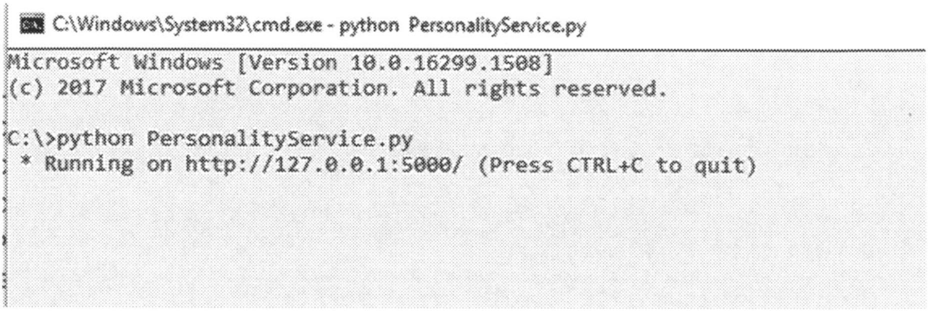

**Figure 4-2.** *Windows command prompt showing the deployment of the service*

## Step 4: Get a Response from the REST API

Now the service is being hosted at the following URL:

```
http://127.0.0.1:5000/getResponse
```

We can check this URL in a REST client (e.g. Postman) with some sample input JSON.

Since Google Dialogflow requires a public URL of your webhook service, we will use Ngrok to generate a public URL corresponding to the local URL that we configured earlier.

Follow these steps to generate a public URL using Ngrok:

1.  To expose a local HTTPS server, download Ngrok from https://ngrok.com/download.

2.  The public URL is available only when the auth token is downloaded from `https://dashboard.ngrok.com` after signing up at `https://ngrok.com/signup`.

3.  The auth token must be specified to Ngrok so that the client is tied to this account. Ngrok saves the auth token at `~/.ngrok2/ngrok.yml` so that there is no need to repeat the previous steps.

4.  Unzip the downloaded Ngrok folder and run the `ngrok.exe` application.

5.  Copy the auth token from the user account to use in the command and run this command at the Ngrok terminal prompt, as shown in Figure 4-3:

```
ngrok authtoken <AUTHTOKEN>
```

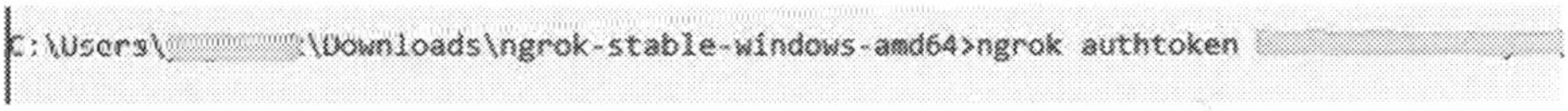

```
C:\Users\          :\Downloads\ngrok-stable-windows-amd64>ngrok authtoken
```

***Figure 4-3.*** *Generating an auth token using Ngrok*

6.  After the previous step, the auth token gets saved to the configuration file, as shown in Figure 4-4.

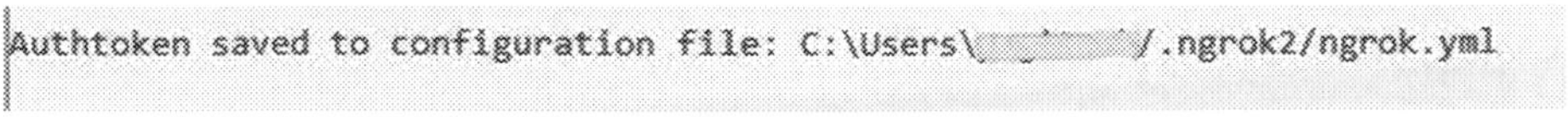

```
Authtoken saved to configuration file: C:\Users\          /.ngrok2/ngrok.yml
```

***Figure 4-4.*** *Saving the auth token*

7.  Ngrok is a command-line application, so use `ngrok http https://<IP>:<PORT>` at the command prompt to expose the HTTPS URL. Here the IP and port correspond to the personality API host and port on which the API is hosted, as shown in Figure 4-5.

C:\Users\ \Downloads\ngrok-stable-windows-amd64>ngrok http https:// :

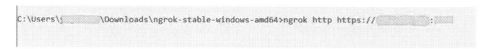

***Figure 4-5.*** *Windows command prompt showing command to expose the HTTPS URL*

8. A new terminal will open after the execution of the command that will display the public URL `https://44e2f215.ngrok.io` corresponding to the local server URL, as shown in Figure 4-6.

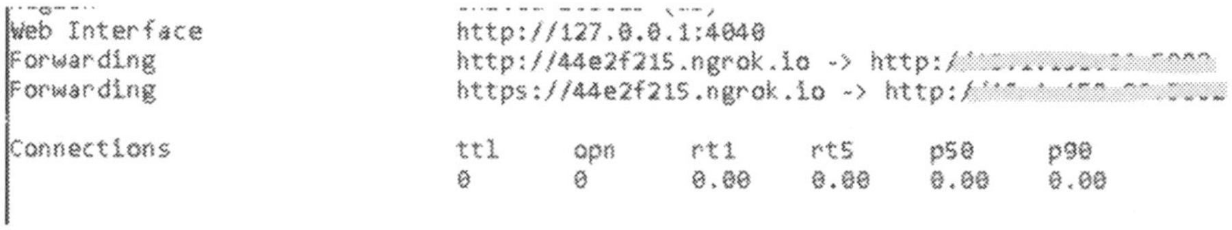
Web Interface http://127.0.0.1:4040
Forwarding http://44e2f215.ngrok.io -> http:/
Forwarding https://44e2f215.ngrok.io -> http:/
Connections ttl opn rt1 rt5 p50 p90
0 0 0.00 0.00 0.00 0.00

***Figure 4-6.*** *Windows command prompt showing public URL*

Now this REST API will be integrated with our webhook service, which integrates the chatbot personality module with Dialogflow.

This deployed API service can be used for a development environment.

For a production environment, the API should be hosted on Apache Server. Refer to the following URL to deploy a service on Apache Server in Windows:

`https://medium.com/@madumalt/flask-app-deployment-in-windows-apache-server-mod-wsgi-82e1cfeeb2ed`

# Linux Server

For Linux, Python 3.6.x and PIP need to be installed in your system before continuing.

## Step 1: Install Flask-RESTful

To install Flash-RESTful, run the following command in the Linux shell, as shown in Figure 4-7:

```
$ pip install flask-restful
```

***Figure 4-7.***  *Linux shell showing installation of Flask-RESTful*

This will install the package and its dependencies.

## Step 2: Build the REST API

Create a `PersonalityService.py` file that will have the personality code that you downloaded from GitHub.

## Step 3: Deploy the Flask REST API

To deploy the REST API service using Flask, run the following command in the Linux shell, as shown in Figure 4-8:

```
$ python PersonalityService.py
```

135

```
10.1.150.55 - PuTTY
adminuser@airo0002:~$ python PersonalityService.py
 * Serving Flask app "PersonalityService" (lazy loading)
 * Environment: production
   WARNING: This is a development server. Do not use it in a production deployment.
   Use a production WSGI server instead.
 * Debug mode: off
 * Running on http://127.0.0.1:5000/ (Press CTRL+C to quit)
```

***Figure 4-8.*** *Linux shell showing deployement of service*

# Step 4: Get a Response from the REST API

Now, the service has been hosted at the following URL:

http://127.0.0.1:5000/getResponse

We can check this URL on a REST client (e.g. Postman) with some sample input JSON that we are going to explain in this section.

Let's see the steps to generate a public URL using Ngrok. The personality API will be hosted on a port on the server or a system via the Apache Server.

1. To expose a local HTTPS server, download Ngrok from https://bin.equinox.io/c/4VmDzA7iaHb/ ngrok-stable-linux-amd64.zip for the Linux server.

2. The public URL is available only when the auth token is downloaded from https://dashboard. ngrok.com after signing up at https://ngrok.com/ signup.

136

3. The auth token must be specified to Ngrok so that the client is tied to this account. Ngrok saves the auth token in ~/.ngrok2/ngrok.yml so that there is no need to repeat this step.

4. Unzip the downloaded Ngrok from a terminal with the following command, as shown in Figure 4-9:

```
$ unzip /path/to/ngrok.zip
```

```
adminuser@airo0002:~$ unzip ngrok-stable-linux-amd64.zip
Archive:  ngrok-stable-linux-amd64.zip
  inflating: ngrok
adminuser@airo0002:~$ ls
```

***Figure 4-9.*** *Linux command for unzipping*

5. Copy the auth token from the user account to the command and run this command at the Ngrok terminal prompt, as shown in Figure 4-10:

```
ngrok authtoken <AUTHTOKEN>
```

```
adminuser@airo0002:~$ ./ngrok authtoken
Authtoken saved to configuration file: /home/adminuser/.ngrok2/ngrok.yml
adminuser@airo0002:~$
```

***Figure 4-10.*** *Linux command to save auth token*

6. After the previous step, the auth token gets saved to the configuration file.

7. Ngrok is a command-line application, so use ngrok http https://<IP>:<PORT> at the terminal prompt to expose the HTTPS URL. Here the IP and port correspond to the personality API host and port on which the API is hosted, as shown in Figure 4-11.

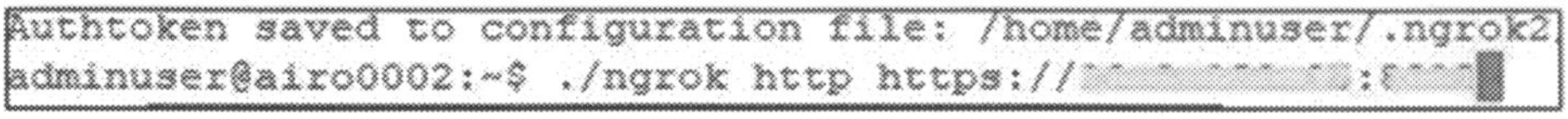

```
Authtoken saved to configuration file: /home/adminuser/.ngrok2
adminuser@airo0002:~$ ./ngrok http https://███████████:█████
```

***Figure 4-11.*** *Linux shell showing command to expose the HTTPS URL*

8.  After the execution of the command, the terminal will display the public URL https://44e2f215.ngrok. io corresponding to the local server URL, as shown in Figure 4-12.

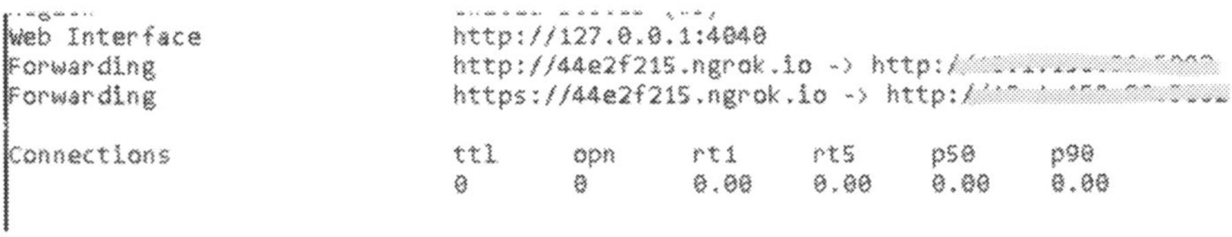

```
Web Interface      http://127.0.0.1:4040
Forwarding         http://44e2f215.ngrok.io -> http://█████████████
Forwarding         https://44e2f215.ngrok.io -> http://█████████████

Connections        ttl      opn      rt1      rt5      p50      p90
                   0        0        0.00     0.00     0.00     0.00
```

***Figure 4-12.*** *Public URL*

For more details, please refer to the Ngrok documentation at `https://ngrok.com/docs`.

This deployed API service is feasible for a development environment.

For a production environment, the API should be hosted on Apache Server. Refer to the following URL to deploy a service on Apache Server in Linux:

`https://www.codementor.io/abhishake/minimal-apache-configuration-for-deploying-a-flask-app-ubuntu-18-04-phu50a7ft`

# Personality JSON

In this section, we'll see the sample request JSON that is supplied on the Dialogflow end and the response JSON that is defined inside the code for our personality webhook service.

First, here's the sample request JSON:

```json
{
  "responseId": "c0c21aff-64c8-4d0b-be9f-d4ad7bff9863-
7e4f1f27",
  "queryResult": {
    "queryText": "What is your Name?",
    "parameters": {},
    "allRequiredParamsPresent": true,
    "intent": {
      "name": "projects/personality-ypunws/agent/
intents/83f25e47-24c0-4fdb-a174-92f7be2394bb",
      "displayName": "Personality"
    },
    "intentDetectionConfidence": 1,
    "languageCode": "en"
  },
  "originalDetectIntentRequest": {
    "payload": {}
  },
  "session": "projects/personality-ypunws/agent/
sessions/67c6b15b-6cbc-a495-8bdd-50bd023f0eb7"
}
```

Now, here's the sample response JSON:

```json
{
    "fulfillmentText": "I am chatbot and answers travel related
queries",
    "fulfillmentMessages": [
        {
            "text": {
                "text": [
```

```
            "I am chatbot and answers travel related
            queries"
        ]
      }
    }
  ],
  "source": "personality-webhook"
}
```

Since our webhook service and chatbot personality API is ready, you can either download the agent file that has the personality use case by accessing the GitHub URL (`https://github.com/dialogflow34/Chat-Bot/tree/master/Chapter_4`) or configure the personality use case by following the steps explained in the "Personality Intent" section.

Import the downloaded agent into Google Dialogflow, as explained in Chapter 2, if you are working with downloaded agent file from GitHub.

# Personality Intent

Now, let's see the steps to create a Personality intent.

1. Create an intent named **Personality** in our Travel agent.

2. Define these training phrases, as shown in Figure 4-13:

   *What is your name?*

   *How are you?*

   *What are you doing?*

   *What is your favorite color?*

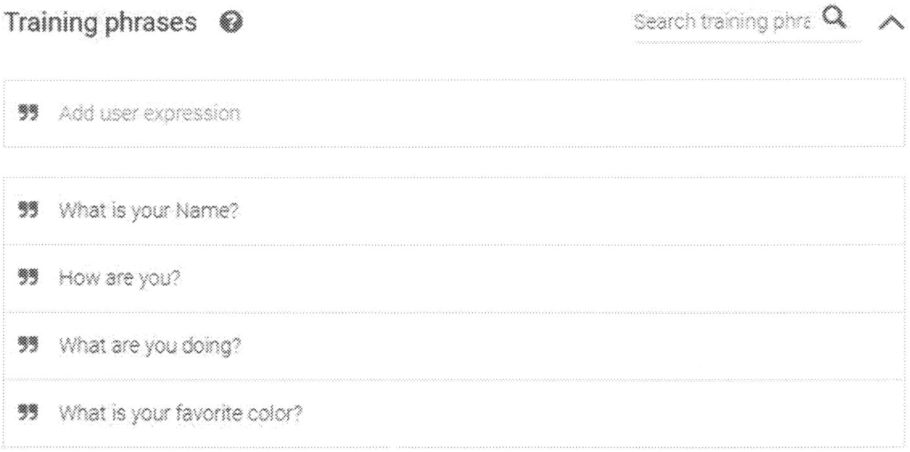

Training phrases  ❓                                    Search training phra  🔍  ⌃

| 💬  Add user expression |
| --- |

| 💬  What is your Name? |
| --- |
| 💬  How are you? |
| 💬  What are you doing? |
| 💬  What is your favorite color? |

***Figure 4-13.*** *Chatbot personality, intent configuration*

Here, we have defined some personality questions in the Personality intent so that it can be passed on to our webhook service, which in turn makes a call to our chatbot personality service for an answer.

Click the toggle button for "Enable webhook call for this intent" for the Fulfillment field of the Personality intent page, as shown in Figure 4-14.

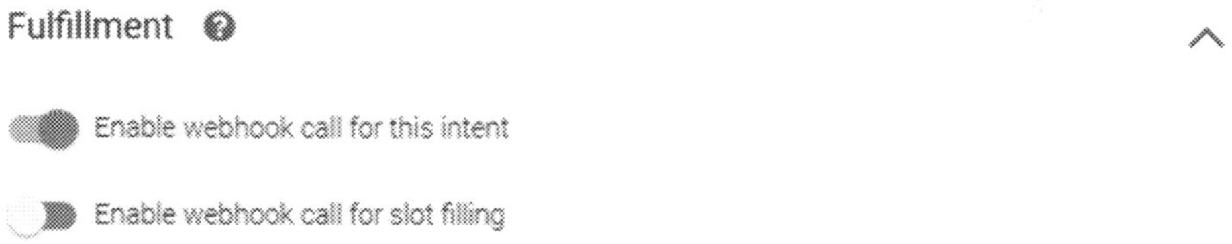

Fulfillment  ❓                                                            ⌃

⬤▬  Enable webhook call for this intent

▬⬤  Enable webhook call for slot filling

***Figure 4-14.*** *Option "Enable webhook call for this intent"*

This enables a webhook call for the Personality intent. Now, go to the left sidebar, click Fulfillment, and then enable the toggle button next to Webhook. Enter the webhook service public URL for the chatbot personality that we configured earlier and click the Save button, as shown in Figure 4-15.

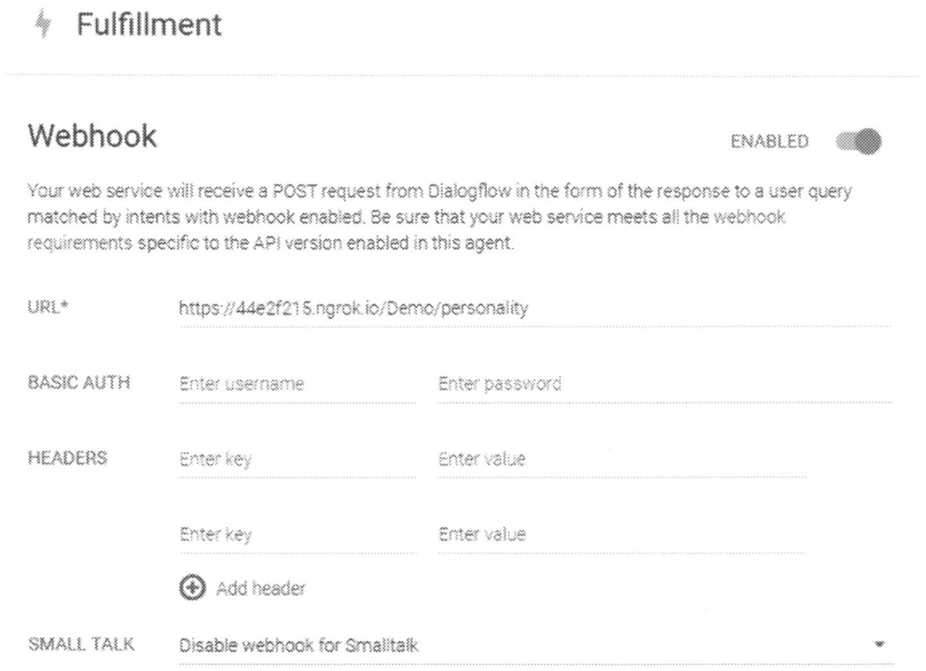

⚡ Fulfillment

---

## Webhook                                                          ENABLED ⬤

Your web service will receive a POST request from Dialogflow in the form of the response to a user query
matched by intents with webhook enabled. Be sure that your web service meets all the webhook
requirements specific to the API version enabled in this agent.

| | |
|---|---|
| URL* | https://44e2f215.ngrok.io/Demo/personality |

| | | |
|---|---|---|
| BASIC AUTH | Enter username | Enter password |
| HEADERS | Enter key | Enter value |
| | Enter key | Enter value |
| | ⊕ Add header | |
| SMALL TALK | Disable webhook for Smalltalk | ▾ |

***Figure 4-15.*** *Integration with chatbot personality*

So, our chatbot personality service via the webhook service using
fulfillment has been integrated with Google Dialogflow.

Now, go to the left sidebar menu and click Integrations. Enable the
toggle button for Web Demo and open the URL in a browser of your
choice.

In Figure 4-16, the user has asked the following personality questions:

- *What are you doing?*

- *What is your favorite color?*

**Figure 4-16.** *Web Demo, chatbot personality*

The system responds with the relevant answer from our webhook service that is integrated with chatbot personality service.

Please note that we can integrate the personality webhook service into any personality service provided by other providers, but we need to ensure that the webhook service processes the input and output JSON in the same format as mentioned earlier.

# Sentiment Analysis

*Sentiment analysis* can be defined as the process of identifying the user's opinion from text. Sentiment analysis plays an important role in responding appropriately to the user. It classifies text into three categories (positive, negative, and neutral) based on the user's opinion of their experience with the services offered. Once we have done that, we can tailor the responses of our chatbot to reflect the sentiment of the user. As an example, if the user is highly negative about something, we can begin by reassuring them or showing concern in our response.

Several NLP providers such as IBM Watson, LUIS, and Google have the capability to perform sentiment analysis on text. Google Dialogflow also has the ability to identify sentiments of the user, but this is applicable only for Enterprise Edition, as shown in Figure 4-17.

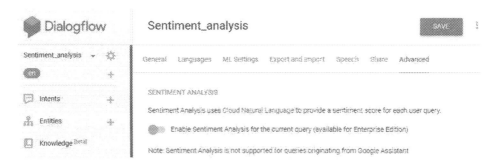

***Figure 4-17.*** *Sentiment analysis in Enterprise Edition*

Here, we are going to show a sample sentiment analysis system that returns the sentiment of the user (i.e., positive, negative, or neutral). This has been exposed as a REST API. You can download the sample sentiment analysis code that has the use case configured for sentiment analysis.

Go to `https://github.com/dialogflow34/Chat-Bot/tree/master/Chapter_4` to download the `Sentiment_Analysis_code.txt` file.

For this book, we have used the Deeppavlov library for the implementation of the sentiment analysis system. This library implements the Google BERT model to train the sentiment analysis system. The Deeppavlov library uses training data in CSV format, where each data point is a pair of sentences and their corresponding opinions (i.e., positive or negative).

For inference, the system processes the user's query and provides the sentiment (i.e., positive or negative) as a response to a query.

We have used the following sample request JSON that is supplied on Dialogflow's end and the response JSON that is defined inside the code for our webhook service (REST API) for sentiment analysis.

Here is the sentiment analysis webhook service request JSON:

```
{
  "responseId": "c0c21aff-64c8-4d0b-be9f-d4ad7bff9863-
7e4f1f27",
  "queryResult": {
    "queryText": "Thanks for your service. But I didn't like
cab options.",
    "parameters": {},
    "allRequiredParamsPresent": true,
    "intent": {
      "name": "projects/personality-ypunws/agent/
intents/83f25e47-24c0-4fdb-a174-92f7be2394bb",
      "displayName": "Sentiment"
    },
    "intentDetectionConfidence": 1,
    "languageCode": "en"
  },
  "originalDetectIntentRequest": {
    "payload": {}
  },
  "session": "projects/personality-ypunws/agent/
sessions/67c6b15b-6cbc-a495-8bdd-50bd023f0eb7"
}
```

Here is the sentiment analysis webhook service response JSON:

```
    {
        "fulfillmentText":   "Sure. We will work with cab
vendor to serve you better in future.",
```

```
            "fulfillmentMessages": [{"text": {
                "text": [
"Sure. We will work with cab vendor to serve you better in
future."                    ]
            }}],
            "source": "Sentiment-webhook"
        }
```

Now, we will explain the complete codebase present in the downloaded file named Sentiment_Analysis_code.txt.

We will start by importing all the required libraries, as shown here:

```
from deeppavlov.core.commands.train import *

from deeppavlov import build_model, configs

from flask import Flask, request, Response

from flask_classful import FlaskView, route

import json

import numpy as np
```

Now, we will define a Python class for the sentiment analysis service, as shown here:

```
class SentimentAnalysis(FlaskView):
```

Next, define the name of the module for reference, as shown here:

```
 module_name = "sentiment_anlysis"
```

Next, to use the sentiment model, use the following function to get a reference from the Deeppavlov library:

```
 MODEL = build_model(module_name, download=False)
```

The value of one argument of this function (i.e., `download`) is `False`. This is required if we don't want the model to be downloaded every time we make a function call to get an instance of the sentiment model.

Because the sentiment analysis system needs to be released as a REST API, we will create an endpoint for the REST API that is used to find the sentiment of the query and return a response to the user.

```
@route("/FetchSentiment", methods=['POST'])
```

Now, this endpoint should be followed by the function that implements the sentiment analysis system, as explained earlier.

```
def run_model_sentiment(self):
```

Declare the required Python variables as shown here:

```
output_json = None

try:

    output_list = list()

    input_list = list()
```

Since the REST API for sentiment analysis receives and processes requests in the user's query from Google Dialogflow in JSON form, the request JSON needs to be parsed to get the user's query, as shown here:

```
json_data = request.get_json(force=True)

input_list.append(json_data["queryResult"]["queryText"])
```

Now, pass the extracted user's query from the request JSON as an argument to the function (i.e., `self.Model()`) that uses the Deeppalov-provided model to find the sentiment of the query, as shown here:

```
if len(input_list) != 0 and input_list[0] != "":

    output_list = self.MODEL(input_list)
```

Next, map the prediction of the model, which is either 0 or 1 with negative and positive, respectively, using the Lambda function of Python, as shown here:

```
output_label = list(map(lambda x: "Positive" if x == "1" \
else "Negative", output_list[0]))

output_score = output_list[1]

score = list(map(lambda x: str(np.max(x)), \
output_score))

output = list(zip(output_label, score))
```

Now, we will generate a response JSON including the sentiment response. Here, the sentiment output should be defined as the value of the key text under the key fulfillmentMessages.

```
output_json = {"fulfillmentText": output,

                "fulfillmentMessages": [{"text": \
                {"text": [output]}}],

                "source": "" \

                }

    except Exception as e:

        print("Error in fetching sentiment for the data\n")

        print(e)
```

Next, return the response JSON to the Google Dialogflow webhook, as shown here:

```
return json.dumps(output_json)
```

You can also use natural language services from any of the cloud vendors such as Google's Cloud Natural Language API (`https://cloud.google.com/natural-language/docs/analyzing-sentiment`) for sentiment analysis. Since Google Dialogflow requires a public URL of our webhook service, we have used Ngrok to generate a public URL corresponding to our local URL, as explained in the previous chatbot personality use case.

The sentiment analysis webhook service integrates with this system to get an opinion and send it to Dialogflow using fulfillment.

Now, to configure the agent, you can either download the agent file (`Sentiment_analysis.zip`) that has the sentiment analysis use case by accessing the GitHub URL (`https://github.com/dialogflow34/ChatBot/tree/master/Chapter_4`) or follow the next steps to configure the use case from scratch.

Import the downloaded agent into Google Dialogflow, as explained in Chapter 2, if you are working with downloaded agent file.

Now, let's see the steps to create a sentiment intent.

Create an intent named **Sentiment** and define these training phrases:

> *Service was good.*

> *I am not satisfied with your services.*

> *I didn't like the options provided by you.*

The Sentiment intent will be added to our Travel agent. It will be used during the feedback stage in our Travel agent. Enable the toggle button "Enable webhook call for this intent," as explained in the earlier personality use case. This enables a webhook call to sentiment analysis. So, whenever the user provides feedback about services, Dialogflow first categorizes the feedback text to the Sentiment intent and then calls the sentiment analysis webhook service, which calls the API to the sentiment analysis system to get an opinion from the feedback text.

- In the left sidebar menu, click Fulfillment and then toggle the button next to Webhook.

- Enter the webhook service URL for sentiment analysis and click the Save button, as shown in Figure 4-18.

⚡ Fulfillment

---

## Webhook                                                ENABLED ⬤

Your web service will receive a POST request from Dialogflow in the form of the response to a user query matched by intents with webhook enabled. Be sure that your web service meets all the webhook requirements specific to the API version enabled in this agent.

| | |
|---|---|
| URL* | https://a3157c60.ngrok.io/Demo/sentiment |
| BASIC AUTH | Enter username          Enter password |
| HEADERS | Enter key          Enter value |
| | ⊕ Add header |
| SMALL TALK | Disable webhook for Smalltalk          ▾ |

***Figure 4-18.*** *Integration with sentiment analysis, webhook*

So, our sample sentiment analysis system via the webhook service using fulfillment has been integrated with Google Dialogflow. Now, go to the left sidebar menu from the sentiment intent page and click Integrations. Enable the toggle button for Web Demo and open the URL in a browser of your choice.

In Figure 4-19, the user has provided feedback (e.g., *I really liked hotel options provided by you*) for hotel options offered by the chatbot. Our travel agent classifies this text into sentiment intent and calls the corresponding sentiment analysis webhook service to get the response text.

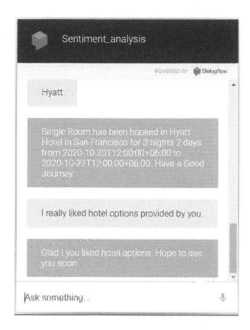

***Figure 4-19.*** *Integration with sentiment analysis, Web Demo*

Please note that we can integrate the sentiment analysis webhook service with any sentiment analysis service, but we need to ensure that the webhook service will process the input and output JSON in the same format as mentioned earlier.

# Event Configuration: Chatbot Transfer

In the previous section, we integrated our Travel agent with sentiment analysis to identify the sentiments of a user from the feedback text. Sentiment identification has another use case as well. Specifically, output from sentiment analysis can be used to transfer a conversation to a human agent if the customer is not satisfied with the responses of our agent.

It also offers flexibility to change responses, to call any third-party APIs, etc. All this can be accomplished using events in Dialogflow.

*Events* in Google Dialogflow are used to trigger an intent not from the end-user expressions but based on the feedback response. We can leverage the same feature for this use case to trigger an opinion-specific intent.

Now, we need to create two intents: one for positive opinions (Issue_resolved) and one for negative opinions (Transfer_to_agent) in our Travel agent.

The user will give feedback to the Travel agent, which will trigger the sentiment analysis intent and call the sentiment analysis webhook service. Then the webhook service processes the input request and calls the sentiment analysis system to extract an opinion from the feedback text, as discussed in previous section and as shown in Figure 4-20.

Now, based on the response from the sentiment analysis system that is either positive or negative, the webhook service will set an event. For example, if the response is positive, then it will set an event to issue-resolved; and for a negative response, it will set a transfer-to-agent event. Once an event has been set, the webhook service generates the JSON response and sends it to Dialogflow via fulfillment.

Fulfillment triggers an intent, either Issue_resolved or Transfer_to_agent, based on the event received from the webhook service and displays a response as defined in the responses section of an intent, either Issue_resolved or Transfer_to_agent.

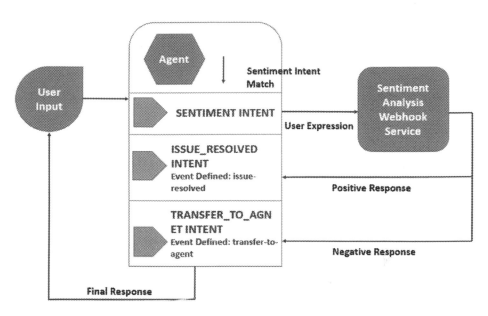

***Figure 4-20.*** *Event configuration, design flow*

1. Create an intent with the name **Issue_resolved**.
   Then, go to the Events section from the Issue_
   resolved intent page.

2. Define the event name as ***issue-resolved***, as shown
   in Figure 4-21.

***Figure 4-21.*** *Event configuration, issue-resolved*

Configure responses for the intent Issue_resolved, as shown in Figure 4-22.

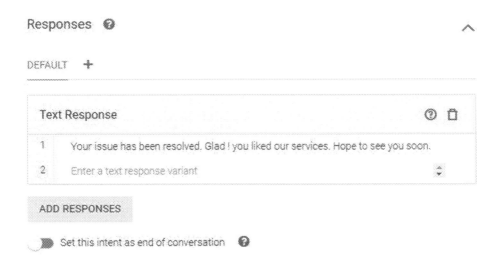

**Figure 4-22.** *Event configuration, Issue-resolved (response configuration)*

Do the same steps for the negative opinion intent (i.e., Transfer_to_agent), as explained earlier. Define an event named **transfer-to-agent**, as shown in Figure 4-23.

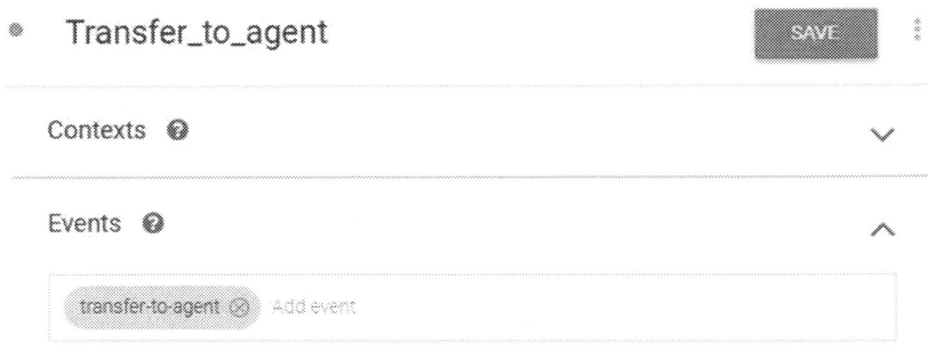

**Figure 4-23.** *Event configuration, Transfer_to_agent*

Configure responses for the intent named Transfer_to_agent, as shown in Figure 4-24.

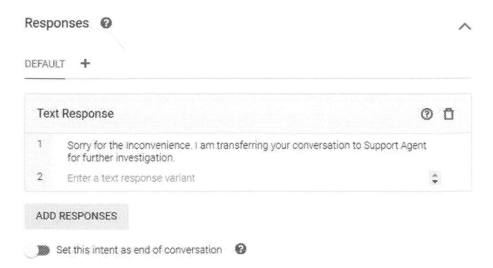

**Figure 4-24.** *Event configuration, Transfer_to_agent (response configuration)*

Here we will be using our existing sentiment analysis webhook service with a small change in the response JSON. Now, the webhook service will send information about events that will trigger an associated intent. The sample request and response JSON is as shown next. As you can see, the webhook service responds with the event name that will be used.

Here's the event configuration for the webhook sample request JSON:

```
{
  "responseId": "c0c21aff-64c8-4d0b-be9f-d4ad7bff9863-
7e4f1f27",
  "queryResult": {
    "queryText": "Thanks for your service. But I didn't like
cab options.",
    "parameters": {},
```

```
    "allRequiredParamsPresent": true,
    "intent": {
      "name": "projects/personality-ypunws/agent/
intents/83f25e47-24c0-4fdb-a174-92f7be2394bb",
      "displayName": "Sentiment"
    },
    "intentDetectionConfidence": 1,
    "languageCode": "en"
  },
  "originalDetectIntentRequest": {
    "payload": {}
  },
  "session": "projects/personality-ypunws/agent/
sessions/67c6b15b-6cbc-a495-8bdd-50bd023f0eb7"
}
```

Here's the event configuration, webhook sample response JSON:

```
{
  "fulfillmentText": "negative",
  "fulfillmentMessages": [
      {
          "text": {
              "text": [
                  "negative"
              ]
          }
      }
  ],
  "source": "Sentiment-webhook",
  "followupEventInput": {
      "name": "transfer-to-agent",
```

```
        "parameters": {},
        "languageCode": "en-US"
    }
}
```

Now, go to the left sidebar menu from the agent page and click Integrations. Enable the toggle button for Web Demo and open the URL in a browser of your choice.

In Figure 4-25, an end user has provided feedback on his experience with our agent. As per the response, user is quite disappointed with the service, so he provided the feedback text *Thanks for your service. But I didn't like cab options.* Our Travel agent classifies this response to the Sentiment intent and calls the sentiment analysis webhook service. The sentiment analysis webhook service processes the input request and calls the sentiment analysis system to extract the sentiment from the feedback text, as discussed in the previous section.

***Figure 4-25.*** *Event configuration, Web Demo*

# Integration with Facebook Messenger

In this section, we will go through the steps to integrate Google Dialogflow with third-party messengers such as Facebook and Slack. This example will help the end user to converse with our agent via Facebook Messenger.

Let's now integrate Google Dialogflow with Facebook Messenger. First we will create the page on Facebook that we are going to use with Google Dialogflow. Follow these steps:

3.  Log in to a Facebook account. Create one if doesn't exists.

4.  Click the Create button and select the Page option. Select the "Community or public figure" section and click the Get Started button, as shown in Figure 4-26.

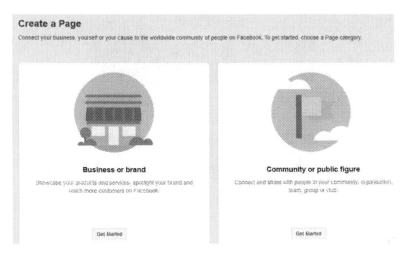

*Figure 4-26.*  *Creating a page*

•  Fill in the required details and name it **Conversation_ Utility**, as shown in Figure 4-27.

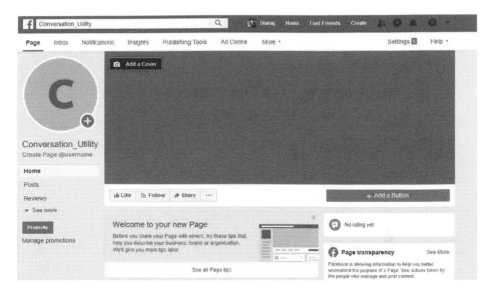

*Figure 4-27.* *Facebook Conversation_Utility page*

- Go to `https://developers.facebook.com/` and log in
  with your Facebook account. It will redirect to the page
  shown in Figure 4-28. Click My Apps in the upper-right
  corner and click Create App.

*Figure 4-28.* *Facebook page for developers*

- Create a new app ID by providing a display name and contact e-mail. For this example, we're using the following:

  **Display Name**: Dialog_flow
  **Contact Email**: dialogflow34@gmail.com

- Click the Create App ID button, as shown in Figure 4-29.

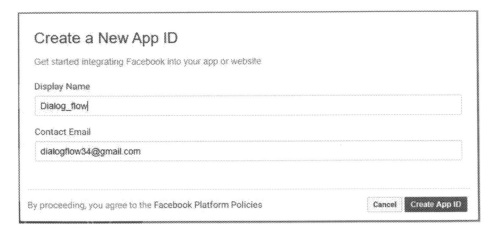

*Figure 4-29.* *Creating an app ID*

- After creation of the app ID, the user will be redirected to the app page, as shown in Figure 4-30.

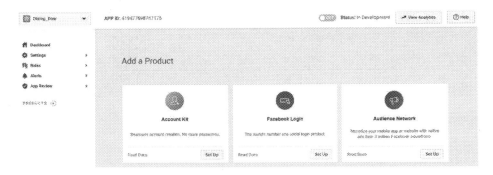

*Figure 4-30.* *Facebook app page*

- Click the Set Up button below the Messenger block to add the product.

- Go to the Token Generation section and click Add or Remove Pages to add a Facebook page, as shown in Figure 4-31.

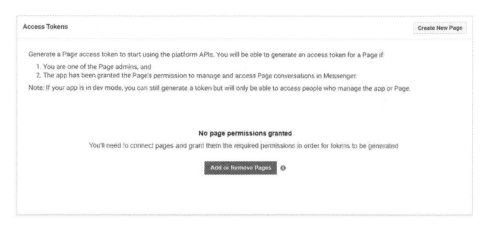

***Figure 4-31.*** *Access Token*

- Select the page Conversation_Utility that we created earlier to integrate with Dialogflow and click the Generate Token button, as shown in Figure 4-32.

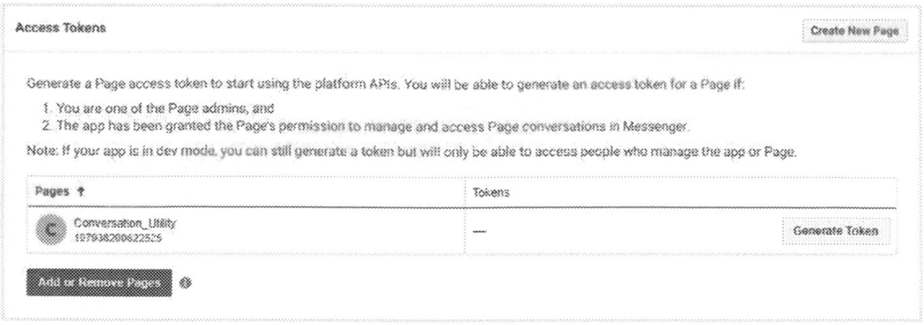

***Figure 4-32.*** *Generating a token for our page*

161

- Copy and save the generated token for further use in Google Dialogflow, as shown in Figure 4-33.

***Figure 4-33.*** *Generated token*

- Open the Google Dialogflow dashboard and go to the left sidebar. Click the Integrations tab and toggle the Facebook Messenger button, as shown in Figure 4-34.

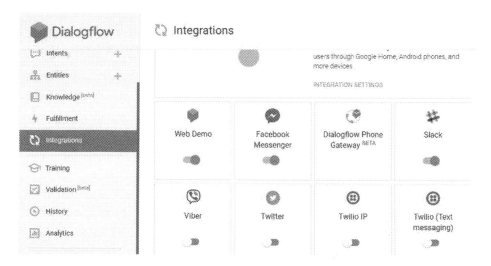

***Figure 4-34.*** *Google Dialogflow integrations*

- This will open a dialog where you can provide a value for the verify token. This can be any string (i.e., facebook-integration).

- Copy the callback URL, which will be required for the Facebook configuration page.

- Paste the copied page access token into the designated field and click the START button, as shown in Figure 4-35.

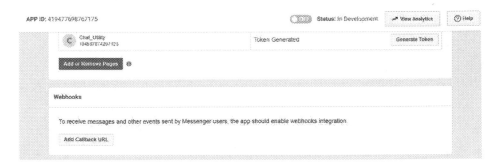

Facebook Messenger

Create and teach a conversational bot for Facebook Messenger.

After you design and test your Dialogflow agent, you can launch your Messenger bot.

1. Get your Facebook Page Access Token and insert it in the field below.
2. Create your own Verify Token (can be any string).
3. Click 'START' below.
4. Use the Callback URL and Verify Token to create an event in the Facebook Messenger Webhook Setup.

More in documentation.

Callback URL    https://bots.dialogflow.com/facebook/afb93bb1-c245-4dde-b8d0-aed5dcdb2da9/webhook

Verify Token    facebook-integration

Page Access    EAAF9g0MS6UcBAHjWc3WVzy08ZCHFfzikw6t3pd2SLmTEa0lo9cdogLsifPICOMubwZCCR9h8(
Token

START

*Figure 4-35.* *Entering the verify token and copying the callback URL*

- Go back to the Facebook app page. Click the Add
  Callback URL under the Webhooks section, as shown in
  Figure 4-36.

APP ID: 419477698767175                Status: In Development    View Analytics    Help

Chat_Utility
1048673742971215               Token Generated              Generate Token

Add or Remove Pages

Webhooks

To receive messages and other events sent by Messenger users, the app should enable webhooks integration.

Add Callback URL

*Figure 4-36.* *Facebook webhook configuration*

- Paste the copied callback URL and verify the token
  name as specified during the integration configuration
  in Google Dialogflow.

- Click the Verify and Save button, as shown in
  Figure 4-37.

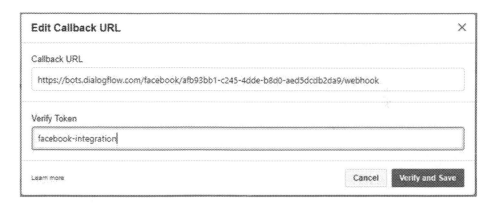

**Figure 4-37.** *Entering the callback URL*

- Click Add Subscriptions for the page name (i.e.,
  Conversation_Utility), as shown in Figure 4-38.

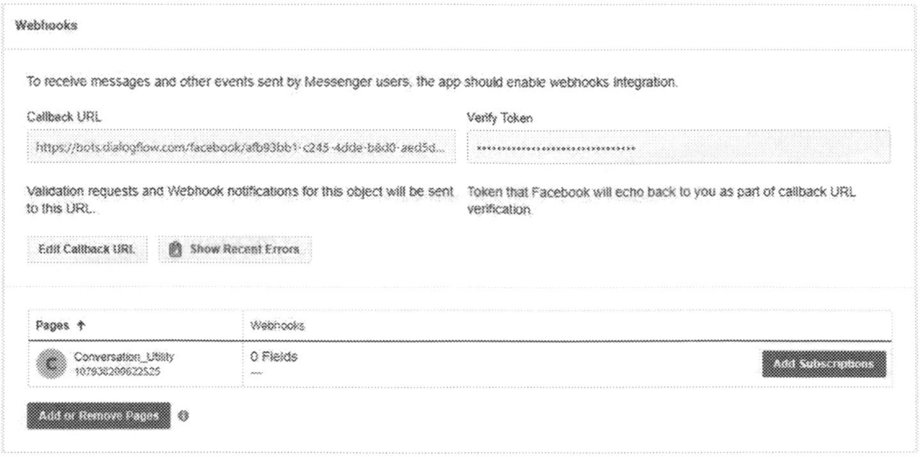

**Figure 4-38.** *Adding subscriptions*

- Select messages and messaging_postbacks under Subscription Fields and click the Save button, as shown in Figure 4-39.

***Figure 4-39.***  *Edit Page Subscriptions dialog*

- Go to the Facebook page, click +Add a Button, and select the radio button corresponding to Send Message under the "Contact you" section, as shown in Figure 4-40.

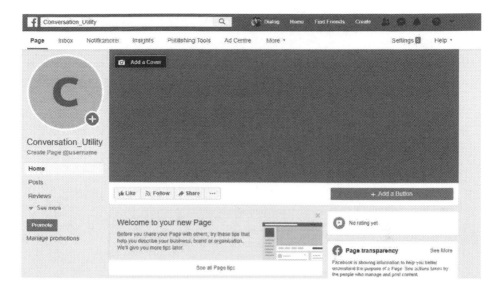

***Figure 4-40.*** *Add button*

- Click the Messenger option and then click the Finish button, as shown in Figure 4-41.

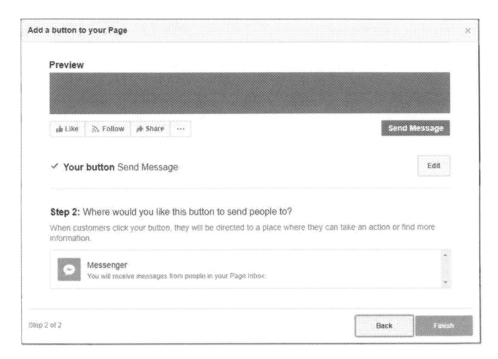

**Figure 4-41.** *Adding a button to our page*

- Click the Test button to check the integration, as shown in Figure 4-42.

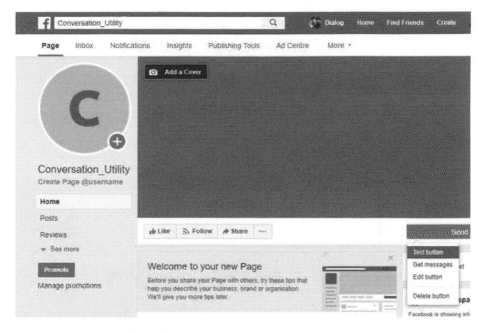

***Figure 4-42.*** *Facebook page*

- This will open Facebook Messenger, and the user can start a conversation, as shown in Figure 4-43.

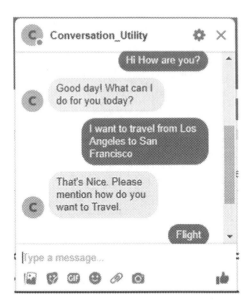

***Figure 4-43.*** *Facebook Messenger integration in action*

# Google Dialogflow's Knowledge Base Integration

In this section, we will implement a document search engine feature in Google Dialogflow.

It is not feasible to define intents and their training phrases for all types of use cases. It works better if we want to perform a specific action, say, fetching weather information for a particular city, finding available hotel accommodations, etc. But for other use cases, say, places to visit anywhere in the United States, it is not possible to define intents for such types of queries. These types of query generally fall into the category of long-tail queries where the answers are within relevant documents.

Google Dialogflow can be integrated with any document search engine service provided by various NLP providers using fulfillment via the webhook service.

Google Dialogflow also has a built-in connector to build a knowledge base where we can upload documents either manually or by specifying a location in cloud storage where the documents exist. The knowledge connector handles the user requests with answers extracted from the uploaded documents. In Google Dialogflow, this is a beta feature, which means it can't be used in a production system. By the time you are reading this book, however, it is possible that the system will be out of beta and ready for use.

In the next sections, we will focus on Google Dialogflow's built-in knowledge connector to build a search engine and integrate it with our Travel agent. Since Google Dialogflow's knowledge base is in beta, we need to enable beta features for our agent.

## Enable Beta Features

To enable beta features, please follow these steps:

1.   Go to the Dialogflow console and select the Travel agent.

2.   Click the settings button next to the agent name, i.e., Travel. Go to the General tab and click the toggle button for "Enable beta features and APIs." Click the Save button to save the changes.

Now, the Google knowledge base plugin has been enabled for our Travel agent, as shown in Figure 4-44.

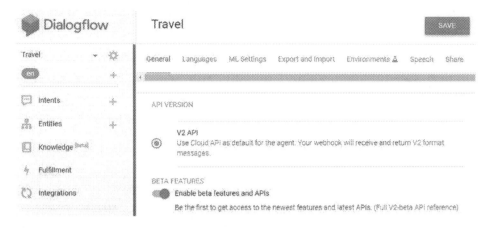

***Figure 4-44.*** *Enabling beta features*

# Create a Knowledge Base

To create a knowledge base, go to the left sidebar menu and click the Knowledge tab.

This will open the Knowledge Bases configuration page, as shown in Figure 4-45.

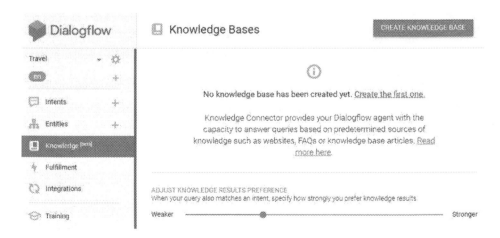

***Figure 4-45.*** *Configuring the knowledge bases*

Follow these steps:

1.  Click the CREATE KNOWLEDGE BASE button.

2.  Fill in the knowledge base name (i.e., **Travel-UseCase**).

3.  Click the SAVE button, as shown in Figure 4-46.

4.  Click the "Create the first one" link to upload documents.

After you name and save this knowledge base, you can add knowledge documents such as websites, FAQs or knowledge base articles.

***Figure 4-46.***   *Naming the knowledge base*

5.  Enter **Places to visit in UK** for Document Name, set Knowledge Type to Extractive Question Answering, set the MIME type to application / pdf.

6.  To upload the documents, choose any option: File on Cloud Storage, URL, or Upload file from your system. Here we will show how to upload a document from our system.

7.  Click the SELECT FILE button and select the files from the system that you want upload to the knowledge base.

8.  Click the CREATE button to finish the configuration, as shown in Figure 4-47.

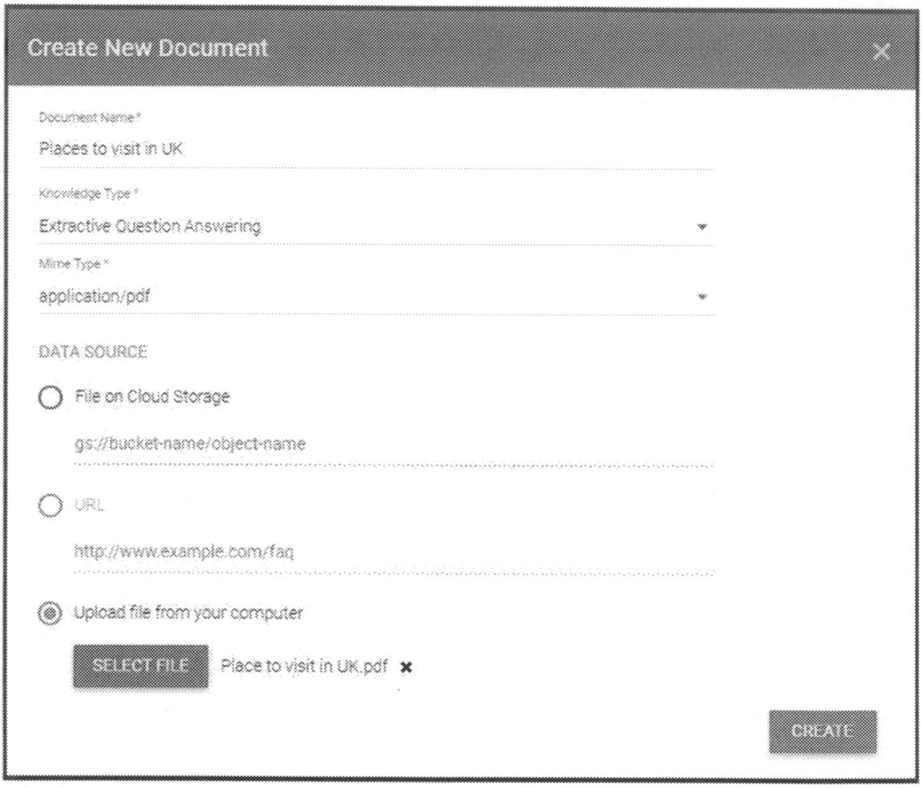

**Figure 4-47.**  *Document upload*

The uploaded documents will be shown as part of your knowledge base, as shown in Figure 4-48.

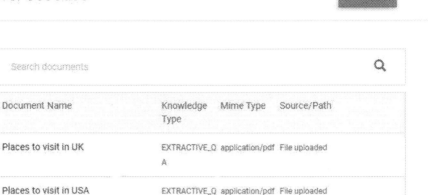

Figure 4-48.  *Document list*

Now, go to the Responses section of the knowledge base and define a response as **$Knowledge.Answer[1]** in the Text Response box, as shown in Figure 4-49.

Responses  ❷                                                          ⌃

DEFAULT  ✚

| Text Response | ⑦  🗑 |
|---|---|
| 1    $Knowledge.Answer[1] | |
| 2    Enter a text response variant | ⬍ |

ADD RESPONSES

⬤ Set this intent as end of conversation  ❷

***Figure 4-49.***  *Knowledge base, response*

Now, if the user asks a question for which no relevant intents exist in our agent, the chatbot will extract the relevant results from our knowledge base.

Next, go to the top-left menu and click the Integrations tab. Toggle the button for Web Demo and open the link in a browser of your choice. Next, enter the query **What are the different places to visit in UK**. You can see our agent has returned results from the knowledge base and not from the intents, as shown in Figure 4-50.

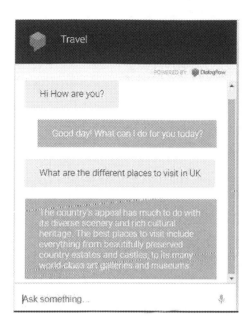

*Figure 4-50.*  *Web Demo, knowledge base*

# Spell Correction

A spell correction feature plays an important role in a chatbot system. This enables a chatbot system to be smart enough to capture spelling mistakes in user queries and responses.

Google Dialogflow provides a built-in spell correction feature. Please note that if there are any spelling mistakes in entity values, they should be corrected by the entity fuzzy matching feature first, before passing the values on to spell correction.

We can also integrate our chatbot with a spelling correction service provided by any other NLP provider using fulfillment via a webhook service that integrates with the spell-check service.

We will start by demonstrating our existing Travel agent without the spell correction feature enabled, where the agent is not able to recognize spelling mistakes.

177

Go to the "Try it now" panel and enter the query **I want to trvl from Los Angeles to Sna Francisco**. Now, the agent is not able to recognize the correct intent because of the misspelled data, so it goes to the fallback intent, as shown in Figure 4-51.

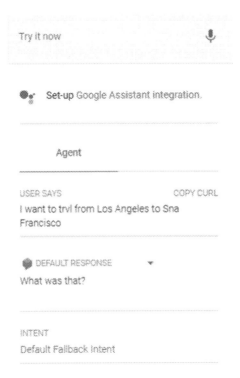

*Figure 4-51.* *Chatbot without spell correction enabled*

To enable spelling correction, click the settings button next to the agent name (i.e., Travel).

Go to the ML Settings tab and click the toggle button under AUTOMATIC SPELL CORRECTION. Then, click the SAVE button, as shown in Figure 4-52.

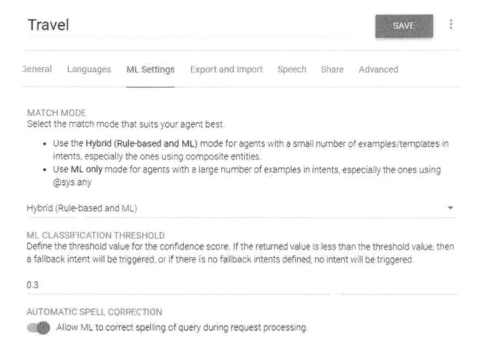

*Figure 4-52.* *Enabling spelling correction*

Now, enter the same misspelled query to see whether the spell correction feature is working or not, as shown in Figure 4-53.

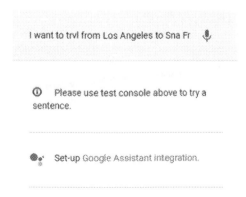

*Figure 4-53.* *Chatbot with spelling correction enabled*

Dialogflow will convert the misspelled query to the correct spelling during request processing and perform intent classification. Now, the correct intent is triggered, and the response comes with that intent, as shown in Figure 4-54.

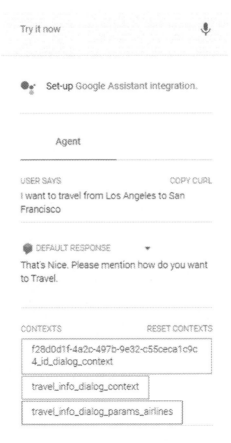

***Figure 4-54.*** *Chatbot response, spell correction*

# Conclusion

In this chapter, we discussed the importance and implementation of chatbot personality. We looked at different scenarios for sentiment analysis such as transfer to a live agent. We also discussed the integration of Google Dialogflow with third-party messengers such as Facebook Messenger. Also, we implemented a document search feature using the Google Dialogflow knowledge base. Finally, we implementing spelling correction in our chatbot.

# CHAPTER 5

# New Research in the Field of Cognitive Virtual Chatbots

Enterprises working on chatbot systems have already started seeing benefits from their deployed cognitive virtual assistants. They are working to implement even more features to enrich conversation systems and improve the user experience.

Some new features such as designing conversations from existing chat logs were impossible just a few short years ago. Today, cloud vendors such as Google and IBM Watson have implemented capabilities in their chatbot systems to recognize intents automatically from existing chat logs; however, this requires chat logs to be in a specific format. In a practical scenario, it is highly unlikely that a chat log follows any specific format. Thus, this feature is still being perfected in the field of chatbot systems.

Another common request from organizations working on a chatbot system is that they want to avoid designing the same use cases across multiple engagements. How do they design one type of use case and then reuse it? Some organizations have been able to address this by designing templates corresponding to use cases and reusing them for other engagements. This also offers the capability to change responses according to the specifics of the new use case.

© Navin Sabharwal, Amit Agrawal 2020
N. Sabharwal and A. Agrawal, *Cognitive Virtual Assistants Using Google Dialogflow*,
https://doi.org/10.1007/978-1-4842-5741-8_5

# Current Research

Increasing demand for chatbot development in various domains, such as e-commerce, healthcare, online booking services, etc., has encouraged new research into some exciting features of chatbot and conversation systems.

These features include generating responses in natural forms, designing an end-to-end conversation flow from an existing conversation's data, generating a response from a bot based on a user's personality, etc.

A multiparty conversation system involves communication between a group of people or multiple systems; these systems tend to have a lot of challenges to processing conversations, including utterance understanding, information search, and reasoning among others. IBM is actively researching this feature and has published some research papers on designing such systems. One paper discusses four important terms that are essential for designing a multiparty conversation system.

- **What**: This means recognizing the intent and entities from the end-user expression.

- **Who**: To whom should it be addressed? Is it a chatbot or user?

- **How**: How should a response be generated? Either it will be a response or an answer from a document.

- **When**: When should a reply be sent? In other words, it will be sent after 10 seconds, 20 seconds, 1 minutes, etc.

Nowadays, chatbots with the capability to generate natural language responses are expected to make conversations more intuitive or human-like. Several patents and research papers exist on this feature, but this is difficult to implement in practice because of the different types of data in existence such as text, audio, images, video, etc. It is also difficult because of a lack of sufficient training data for various domains such as healthcare, insurance, etc. One of the patents uses the concept of how an individual communicates with the chatbot system and learns structure from those conversations to generate responses. Therefore, you may see different response text for the same query from different users, but all responses will have the same meaning.

The current implementations of cognitive virtual chatbots (CVAs) lack the capability to generate an end-to-end conversation flow from chat logs and to automatically generate dialogue. This is the most important research area, and most of the big industry players are actively working on the topic. One of the patents in this area implements this by analyzing conversation flows to understand the meaning of each line of text and by connecting each distinct response from both sides to finally generate conversation flows. The same approach can be used in spoken dialogue systems to automatically generate dialogue.

In current CVA systems, goal-oriented dialogue agents are generally trained to complete a specific goal. For any other new task, you may not find a dataset consisting of human-to-chatbot interactions. In such cases, a dialogue developer will need to develop this from scratch for all possible interactions. This is a time-consuming process and requires continuous support from developers. This problem has been well studied by Google, and its AI track has introduced a new framework known as machine-to-machine (M2M) that automates the generation of an end-to-end dialogue agent for goal-oriented systems. As an example, CVA developers now can use an existing dialogue agent to generate a new dialogue agent for tasks such as booking an online appointment.

# Research Acquisitions

A lot of research in the AI field for chatbots is being led by various startups, and some of these good ideas have been acquired by industry majors. Deepmind, the creators of AlphaGo, was acquired by Google in January

2014, for $500 million. Some of its cutting-edge technologies have now been integrated into Google Assistant. Another example is that Siri was acquired by Apple in 2010 to enable virtual assistant capabilities in iPhones. Further examples include Wit.ai, which was acquired by Facebook, and Maluuba, which was acquired by Microsoft, to expand their AI ecosystems.

Research in the area of human conversations is an exciting and active field where every day new discoveries are being made and new technologies are being implemented to make cognitive virtual agents better. The day is not far that we will not be able to distinguish a CVA from a human being.

# Index

## A

Action field, 22–25, 41, 44, 56
Agent
    access configuration, 93
    advanced features, 93
    configuration, 95
    deleting, 86
    Dialogflow, 18
    language, 87
    list of, 101
    settings, 84
    training, 79–81
    voice configuration, 92
AI Platform, 7, 10
Allow automated expansion
    option, 39
API Keys, 86
API Version setting, 85

## B

Batch operations, 29–30
Beta features, 85, 171–172

## C

Chatbot personality
    definition, 119
    extract_word function, 125

find_similar_response function,
    128, 129
intent, 140–143
JSON, 138–140
Linux Server
    deploying flask REST API, 135
    Flask-RESTful,
      installation, 135
    get response, 136–138
    REST API, 135
local URL, 130
module, 122
MongoDB database, 123
natural language
    processing–based
    retrieval model, 120
NLP tasks, 124
parameters, 123
predefined and user-defined
    packages, 121
punct_tokenize function, 125
Python class, 121
spell_checker function, 126
subfolders/packages, 120
Windows Server
    deploy flask REST API, 132
    Flask-RESTful,
      installation, 130, 131

© Navin Sabharwal, Amit Agrawal 2020
N. Sabharwal and A. Agrawal, *Cognitive Virtual Assistants Using Google Dialogflow*,
https://doi.org/10.1007/978-1-4842-5741-8

Printed in the United States
By Bookmasters